D1592553

Why I Am An Atheist

One of a series of lectures delivered by Madalyn O'Hair at:

University of Maryland
Temple University
University of Hawaii
Rice University
U.C.L.A.
Southern Methodist University
University of Illinois
Loyola University
St. Edward's University
Harvard University
University of Houston
University of Pennsylvania
Howard University
Northeastern University
Dartmouth College
Drake University
University of Indiana
University of Texas
University of Arkansas
University of Ohio
University of Nebraska
University of Colorado
University of Utah
University of New Jersey
University of Florida
University of South Carolina
University of Michigan
(and to many other groups)

Why I Am An Atheist

including
A History of Materialism

Second Revised Edition

by
Madalyn O'Hair, J.D.

American Atheist Press
Austin, Texas   1991

American Atheist Press, P.O. Box 140195, Austin, TX 78714-1095

© 1966, 1980, 1991 by American Atheist Press
Published 1966. Second Revised Edition 1991
Printed in the United States of America

Library of Congress Cataloging-in-Publication Data

O'Hair, Madalyn Murray
    [Why I am an atheist]
    Why I am an atheist ; including, A history of materialism / by
Madalyn O'Hair.—2nd ed. rev.
    p.   cm.
    Includes index.
    ISBN 0-910309-98-1 : $6.00
    1. Atheism. 2. Materialism—History. I. O'Hair, Madalyn Murray.
History of materialism. 1991. II. Title: Why I am an atheist.
III. Title: History of materialism.
BL 2747.3.O363   1991   91-26426
221'.8—dc20   CIP

To Pup

Contents

About the Author

I t is doubtful if there is anyone in the United States who does not know the name Madalyn O'Hair. She is probably the best-known Atheist in the world today.

Lawyer, researcher, author, speaker, organizer, businesswoman, she is the founder of American Atheists, Inc., American Atheist Women, American Atheist GHQ, American Atheist Library and Archives, Inc., American Atheist Press, "American Atheist [Television] News Forum," "American Atheist Radio Series," Society of Separationists, Inc., *American Atheist* magazine, and cofounder with GORA (Goparaju Rama-chandra Rao of India) of the international United World Atheists, and first co-organizer of the triannual World Atheist Meet held in India in 1972.

Beginning her career in her father's contracting business, she has worked as an office manager, as both a civil and an aerodynamics engineer, as a psychiatric social work supervisor, as a supervisor in family and children's agencies and in probation departments and welfare agencies, as a union organizer, and as a college instructor. Her primary legal work was with the Social Security Administration of the Health, Education and Welfare Department of the United States. During World War II, from 1943 to 1946, she served as a commissioned officer in the Women's Army Auxiliary Corps and the Women's Army Corps in the United States, Africa, and Europe (primarily Italy and France) on the cryptographic staff in Supreme Allied Headquarters.

After the war she was intensively involved in disarmament, peace, desegregation, and union organization activities. She was a major opponent of Sen. McCarthy during the era of "un-American" concepts. An early proponent of "feminism," taking her cue from her grandmother, Alice McHenry Mays, she advocated equal wages for women beginning in the 1930s. Dr. O'Hair actively opposed the war in Vietnam during the time of the French administration there and before the United States intervention, organizing speakers and debates years before the fall of Dien Bien Phu, which eliminated the French. She also opposed the "police action" in Korea, the testing of nuclear weapons in the atmosphere, the suppression of the rights of the Algerians and the South Africans. She worked actively to change the lot of migrant workers, foster home care recipients, inmates of detention centers, and children offenders of the law.

Beginning her fight for the civil libertarian rights of American Atheists and state/church separation in 1959, she is the person most responsible for the current situation whereby Bible reading and prayer recitation are barred from the public schools of the United States.

That was the beginning of a series of legal battles which has often centered around prayer as she fought to stop the prayers of astronauts in space, to stop prayers at governmental functions, to remove the phrase "under God" from the Pledge of Allegiance, the motto "In God We Trust" from the currency, and "So help me God" from court oaths. In addition, one of her most famous suits was to stop the pope from performing a Roman Catholic mass on the Washington mall in our nation's capital. She has fought to tax the earnings of church businesses, church lands, and to stop any subsidy by government to the churches. Her cases in the 1980s focused on the judicial system of the state of Texas, which she challenged as "unconstitutionally constituted" since all Atheists and agnostics are precluded from holding any office or public trust in that state, by Texas constitutional fiat. She also has sought to remove both religious crosses and crèches (nativity scenes) from any governmental property, all religious holidays from public schools, and to stop any governmental financial assistance to church-related schools or institutions.

For over two decades she has been a staple on television and radio talk shows, seen often on those of Johnny Carson, Phil Donahue, Tom Snyder, and David Hartman, to name a few. Her university appearances include Harvard, Dartmouth, Temple, Drake, Rice, Southern Methodist and the universities of Maryland, Hawaii, Illinois, Iowa, Houston, Utah, Texas, Arkansas, Ohio, Nebraska, Colorado, Michigan, etc.

Dr. O'Hair, whose graduate degrees are in psychiatric social work and law — with a doctorate in jurisprudence — is currently most involved in the legal theoretics and the administrative necessities for the upcoming founding of the first American Atheist University and is now positing the legal base for an American Atheist Civil Liberties Union.

She is the retired president of the parent organization at the American Atheist GHQ, where her son Jon Murray is the current president. American Atheists maintains a network of activists and spokespersons across the nation, in order to protect the interests of Atheists at a local level. A coequal in the family triumvirate is her daughter, Robin Murray-O'Hair, who, as its president, presides over the American Atheist Library and Archives, now the largest holding of Atheist material in the world.

Dr. O'Hair is listed in *Who's Who in the World, Who's Who in America, Who's Who in Religion, World's Who's Who of Women, Personalities of the South,* and *Dictionary of International Biography.*

Her books include: *Why I Am an Atheist, What on Earth Is an Atheist!, An Atheist Epic, The Atheist World, An Atheist Speaks, Atheist Heroes, Let Us Prey, An Atheist Primer, An Atheist Looks at Church Wealth, Freedom from Religion, The Atheist Plea, Atheists: The Last Minority, Atheism in the United States, The Religious Factors in the War in Vietnam, An Original Theory in Respect to the Origin of Religion, Jesus Christ — Super Fraud, Religious Games People Play,* and *Short History of American Atheism.* She was also the advisory editor for the *New York Times's* Arno Press in its twenty-five-volume set *The Atheist Viewpoint.*

Dr. O'Hair has two sons, William J. and Jon Garth Murray, the latter of whom has enthusiastically joined her in the Atheist enterprises she founded. Her daughter, Robin Eileen Murray-O'Hair, is the editor of the *American Atheist* magazine.

Since the beginning of 1980, she most frequently requests that her son, Jon Murray, take any television, radio, or college/university appearances. See informational document on Jon Garth Murray, president of American Atheists, last page of this booklet.

Mrs. O'Hair's office is at the American Atheist GHQ, 7215 Cameron Rd., Austin, TX 78752-2973, mailing address P.O. Box 140195, Austin, TX 78714-0195. Telephone: 512-458-1244.

Introduction

I n 1961 in the midst of the legal fight for the removal of reverential Bible reading and unison prayer recitation from the public schools in Baltimore, Maryland, I was asked to address the student body at the University of Maryland. At that time, I composed a speech, which is reproduced here.

I have always been aware of the cadence, the rhythm, the verbal emphasis given in speaking and have written my speeches to accommodate to them, to my own individual style of delivery, and to what I want to emphasize and how I want to emphasize it.

I am a powerful speaker and well aware of the fact.

I spoke at 8:00 P.M. that evening in 1961. I had tailored what I had to say to last approximately one hour. The hall was jammed with students, all seats taken, many of them leaning against the walls, squatting cross-legged on the floor. The "question and answer" session began immediately after the speech and lasted until 3:00 A.M. the following morning.

It may be that I was the first person in the United States to give a speech on Atheism at any college or university. Later I was astonished that I could use the same speech over and over again at some of the most prestigious universities and have the same reactions from the students. During the next ten years I wrote, and delivered, other speeches — but this was a perennial favorite, and I knew that I could give it anytime, anywhere and draw the same astonishing results.

Then, in June 1963, the Supreme Court of the United States issued a decision in the case of *Murray v. Curlett,* which held that Bible reading and prayer recitation in the public schools were impermissible under

1

the doctrine of separation of state and church articulated in the First Amendment to the Constitution of the United States. The decision caused an enormous interruption in the life of my family, for the nation exploded with such anger and hatred that it was necessary to flee from the continental United States for fear of our lives.

Within several years we were able to reestablish in Austin, Texas. Although I was still much "on the road" making television, radio, college, and university appearances, it became possible, slowly, to attempt to print and distribute the beginnings of modern Atheism which I was putting together. The first such item printed, in 1966, was the speech that I had given at the University of Maryland. At the time I did not know that the publication of this speech was the beginning of the American Atheist Press.

There was quite a demand for the little booklet, which still retained the title which I had given to the speech back in 1966, and it went through six editions, each one having a new cover, each of which was just as dreadful.

In 1990, Miss Robin Murray-O'Hair, who was then in charge of all book production for the American Atheist Press, told me that a new edition of the speech was needed and that it was necessary for me to look at the prior editions since there were many accretions thereto which she did not think were mine.

She furnished all six editions to me, with page comparison layouts four feet long, glued one to another. When I saw what had happened in the years 1966 to 1990, I was horrified. Proofreaders, copy editors, keyboard inputters had simply added, changed, or amended as suited their little brains, and what was being distributed as the speech which I had given was so mutilated, distorted, and modified that I did not recognize it.

Fortunately along the way, a copy of each edition had been preserved in the American Atheist Library and Archives and I was able to return to the original.

And what you have in your hands is it.

This is a historical document, for no one else had ever had the courage to stand up in front of hundreds of earnest students and say what I had said. I have decided that I want that preserved.

Since I made the speech I have learned a helluva lot. At that time I knew little or nothing about Atheism because there was little or nothing available, in public libraries, college or university libraries, or anywhere else. There still is little or nothing available as the librarians in the library systems of the United States continue their hostility to Atheism, either refusing Atheist books and magazines, or disposing of any that they find lurking on their shelves.

The amazing part of this is that the speech is still good, is still an introduction to Atheism for anyone who desires to look. It is in clear, unambiguous language, written — and presented — so as to be simple, easily understood, and powerful in impact.

The speech has served Atheism well. I tender it to you forthwith as a learning experience.

Madalyn O'Hair
Austin, Texas
August 13, 1990

Why I Am an Atheist

I have composed these two speeches because I want to talk with you. I want to talk with you because I have something to say.

My name is Madalyn Murray O'Hair.

I am an Atheist.

I am a bit more than that — an Atheist. I am, in fact, **the** Atheist. The Atheist who made Americans stop to take a little stock of their accepted values. For I am the Atheist who fought a battle right up to and through the Supreme Court of the United States in order to have Bible reading and prayer recitation, as a religious ceremony, removed from the public schools in all fifty states of our Union.

Two questions are put to me more than any others, and they are "How did you get that way?" and "Why do you want to fight about it?"

Do you want to know first how I got that way or the really exciting story of why I am fighting in the courts of the land for what I accept?

All right, perhaps I will tell you how I got that way. But first, what way did I get? Let's make it plain right from the start what an Atheist is or what an Atheist is not.

First, I am not an agnostic, nor a rationalist, nor a realist, nor a secularist, nor humanist, nor any other fancy name behind which people must hide in order to be safe in our society. And isn't it an indictment against our society that we who do not believe — we nonbelievers of all stripes — must hide behind certain names since reprisals and sanctions would be put into effect against us if we said what we really believe?

For years our own family functioned after an old-fashioned philosophy handed down from my grandparents' grandparents. It was a very nice homey philosophy of "Shake your fist in your pocket, never shake your fist in someone's face." Never say what you really think. Many more families in America, apparently, have had the same philosophy and lived by it. For today everyone keeps their hands in their pockets and their tongues in their cheeks until we are a nation of liars and deceivers, afraid to say what we really think.

Well, I am neither afraid nor ashamed to say what I think. I am an Atheist, and this means, *at least*, that I do not think there is $\underline{a}$ god or $\underline{any}$ god, personal or in nature or manifesting himself, herself, or itself in any way. I do not think there is such a thing as heaven or hell or perdition or purgatory, or any of the stages in-between going up, down, or in any other direction. I do not think there is any life after death. I do not accept miracles. I do not accept the concept of angels. I do not accept prophets, and I do not accept any holy book of any kind, be it the Bible, the Torah, the Veda, the Koran, the Upanishads, the Oahspe, the Urantia, or any other book, in any age in the history of man, whether it was written by Moses, Mary Baker Eddy, Joseph Smith, Mohammed, Gautama Buddha, or the fickle finger of fate.

I do not accept any man as holy, and this includes any so-called savior from Moses to Jesus Christ, Mohammed or his daughter Fatima, the angel Moroni, the popes or any oracles, self-appointed or appointed by other persons — or any alleged gods. I do not accept that there is efficacy in prayers said either by yourself, myself, a priest, a rabbi, a minister, a guru, or your mother.

Please, as adults we must face that this is *silly.* These ancient fables and ideas are silly, and we no longer need to cling to them. Do you really believe any woman can have a child without a sexual relationship? This is an insult to you and me. It is an insult to our intelligence and to our common sense and to our own experience which we have gained from living.

Well, that is what I don't accept. A charge against any Atheist is that we are negative, that we do *not* "believe" and that we should have a positive program. Therefore, many people ask us, "What is your positive approach to the problems of man, of man living in human relationships, in a hard, cruel world?"

Now this isn't corny because it *is* a hard and cruel world. The most difficult thing in the world to do is to live and to get along with other people, to earn a living, to meet our basic needs. It is very difficult to do this. You have a hard time doing it and so do I; we need a decent, modern, sophisticated, and workable set of standards by which we can get along with ourselves and with others. We can toss out all this old garbage of rules laid down by god. No god ever gave _any_ man _any_ thing and never will. We solve our problems ourselves or they are not going to get solved, and you know it and I know it.

When we became involved in the suit to take Bible reading and prayer recitation out of the public schools of our nation, we did a unique thing. We went to a court of this land, and for the first time in the history of the United States it was stated in a court and in a legal brief that we objected to Bible reading and prayer recitation because _we were Athe-ists_. We did not say that our family was Jewish and did not, therefore, accept the New Testament. We did not say that we were Roman Cath-olics and did not, therefore, accept the King James Version of the Bible. We did not say that we were Buddhists or Mohammedans and could not accept the Christian practice. We said that we were Atheists, liv-ing in a modern world and that we did not accept any of these fairy tales of any kind. The attorney said to me, "OK, Mrs. Murray, if you want to base your suit on Atheism and Atheism alone, then you write up a little blurb about what an Atheist is and I'll put it into the suit."

So — I did and he did and this is it.

For the first time in any law books, in any history books, you can go and read it for yourself. It is in the records of the Baltimore, Maryland, Superior Court in the case of _William J. Murray III v. John N. Curlett._[1] William Murray III is my oldest son, and John N. Curlett was the pres-ident of the Board of School Commissioners of Baltimore City. The case was filed in December 1960, and it reached the United States Supreme Court for argument in February 1963. The statement to which I refer says, and you will understand this despite the legal terminology here and there:

> Your petitioners are Atheists and they define their life-style as follows. An Atheist loves himself and his fellow man instead of god. An Atheist knows[2] that heaven is something for which we should

---

[1] _Murray v. Curlett,_ 374 U.S. 203, 83 S.Ct. 1560, 10 L.Ed. 2d. 844 (1963).
[2] In the original petition the verb _believe_ was used throughout. In this edition that word is replaced by "think" or "accept." I propose that the use of the verb "to believe" be eschewed for general use since its dic-tionary definition is (a) to have a firm religious faith, (b) to accept on faith.

Faith, of course, is belief and trust in, or loyalty to, god.

7

work now — here on earth — for all men together to enjoy. An Atheist thinks that he can get no help through prayer but that he must find in himself the inner conviction and strength to meet life, to grapple with it, to subdue it and enjoy it. An Atheist thinks that only in a knowledge of himself and a knowledge of his fellowman can he find the understanding that will help to a life of fulfillment.

Therefore, he seeks to know himself and his fellowman rather than to know a god. An Atheist knows that a hospital should be built instead of a church. An Atheist knows that a deed must be done instead of a prayer said. An Atheist strives for involvement in life and not escape into death. He wants disease conquered, poverty vanquished, war eliminated. He wants man to understand and love man. He wants an ethical way of life. He knows that we cannot rely on a god nor channel action into prayer nor hope for an end of troubles in a hereafter. He knows that we are our brothers' keepers and keepers of our own lives; that we are responsible persons, that the job is here and the time is now.

Doesn't that sound serious and intense? Well, we really are persons who subscribe to the "do it yourself" idea. You know that we could knock tuberculosis completely off the map within two years if we gave a concentrated national effort to it. Science has already (substantially) vanquished diphtheria. We won't ever do it by praying. The churches are never going to bother themselves with tuberculosis — except to have certain evangelicals claim that they can cure it with the laying on of hands and the acceptance of money. The mainline churches are much too interested in seeing that everyone gets to heaven when they die than to help prevent anyone from dying.

Getting to heaven: we Atheists are not charlatans who promise "pie in the sky." We tell you frankly that the only happiness, the only fulfillment, the only total living you will ever have is right here and right now. You will get somewhere only with well-thought-out planning and hard work that you do. No one is involved in helping you but you.

Well, you say, that statement which you put into your suit sounds like everything that everybody really wants, so you are no different than we are. Well, you're right in a way. We are knowledgeable, we Atheists. We try to find some basis of rational thought on which we can posit our actions and our life-style and we have it. It has existed for thousands of years and it antedates Christianity, which is only about sixteen hundred years old.

We accepted the technical philosophy of materialism. Aha! you think

8

ritus and revered by the ancients for having liberated man from fear of a god and for asserting the validity of science, was for two thousand years anathematized by leaders of the church who falsely depicted him as an enemy of morality and a disseminator of vice. The advocates of idealism, or "idea-ism" as I like to think of it, sought to slander materialism, to equate it with pure hedonism and a selfish, purposeless way of life which caters only to gluttony and wasteful living with no respect for nature, material resources, or other forms of life, animal or plant.

Materialism, read it, you can see for yourself through all the lies which are heaped upon it to hide it. Materialism is the philosophy of life according to rational processes. The intellectual and other capacities of the individual are to be developed to the highest degree in a social system where this is encouraged. We do not have such a social system now.

Well, where does man really fit into this? you say. Are you a humanist? Do you think that man is an exceptional unique being although not of divine origin and he, man, is the center of your philosophical system?

Materialists, and we call ourselves Atheists, do not accept the divinity of man. Because of this we shy away from systems of thought which exalt the human animal. We are embarrassingly aware that we are most insignificant. We are more insignificant than the sea or the wind on our planet alone. Man must share the earth with all other animals. *And we are animals.* We must share the earth also with the earth's resources. Naturally, therefore, a materialist is not an exploiter of man or nature. A materialist is neither an accumulator nor a wasteful user nor a conspicuous consumer and least of all does he revel in the glorification of man.

"Well," you say, "how does this fit in with living day by day? Do you live by the Golden Rule?" No, I don't like the Golden Rule, and you know what the Golden Rule is these days. It is "Do unto others what they would do unto you — but do it first." Personally, I try to live by what is called the categorical imperative. "The *what?* What's that?" you say. Well, we have the writings of Immanuel Kant,[5] a philosopher who lived in the eighteenth century. He struggled with ideas of rules of conduct and ideas of morality. He came up with three suggestions. One was that we should treat every other person and ourselves as "ends" and not as "means." That is, we should treat ourselves and others as ends in themselves and not as means to an end. You just try that one. I've tried to

---

[5]Immanuel Kant (1724–1804), German philosopher.

11

keep this rule for thirty years[6] and I break it all the time. It is a very exacting idea by which to try to live.

Kant's second suggestion was to so act that any of your actions could be made into universal laws. That's something. Cheat that poor Joe out of a nickel and then have a universal law that everyone always cheats everybody else out of a nickel, including you.

His third suggestion was to search for truth. Well, I just gave up on that one. I don't know if we'll ever find out what truth is or what it isn't. We have the burden of trying. [The Moslems felt that truth was in holy wars.] The Roman Catholic church said that truth was to exterminate hundreds of thousands of persons in the Inquisition. [Even here in the United States, the colonists killed witches, didn't they?] So I have amended his third suggestion to "seek knowledge" — keep on a quest to find out as much as you can about everything. Test everyone's word. Truth will survive such a test. So quest and test for yourself.[7]

Well, let's pause here for just a minute. I know what you are going to say now. You're going to say, "Well, that's all well and good, but you have not proved that god does not exist; you're just talking." All right, so let me take you back to the rules of logic and logical argument, because if we're going to get anywhere we must have some rules of the game. We all agree, you and I, all of the religious people, all the Atheists. We all agree on one rule which I give you now. That is: when anyone postulates a theory, he has the burden of proof of that theory. And I mean by that that when Newton said he had discovered a theory which later came to be recognized as a law of nature — the theory of gravity — he had the *burden of proof*. It was necessary for him to prove that his theory was correct. Well, now, it's hard to believe but religious leaders, religious scholars, and churchmen of every kind have admitted that a god is only a theory. They have admitted this because they keep putting forth more and different proofs constantly to support their "god" theory. If a god really was, they wouldn't need to put out all these

---

[6]The original speech was written in 1961, at which time Mrs. O'Hair was forty-two years old.

[7]Since the time of the writing of this speech, Mrs. O'Hair has asked Atheists everywhere to use the ordinary legal test of "a reasonably prudent man" in their conduct. Such a person knows the consequence of his actions and lives in such a way that those consequences are not detrimental either to himself or to society.

arguments and theories. For thousands of years they have argued this point, and the burden of proof is on them and they know it.

We Atheists have evaluated their arguments, and we merely decide if we want to accept them or reject them. So, any good Atheist simply acquaints himself with all of these arguments that have gone on for thousands and thousands of years.

This is impossible, you say.

Well, it will surprise you to hear that in thousands of years religionists have only come up with five basic arguments. Five! Why would anyone need five reasons to believe? And isn't it curious that every religious person says, "I believe in a god," rather than "god is." This only reflects that god is still a theory.

You're getting impatient. What are the possible sources of belief in the existence of a god? *First*, there is a direct sensory experience. This is real or imagined. Have you seen god? Well, if you have never seen him, you know no one else ever has, because you can trust your own senses. [If the god idea is a "universal," everyone should be able to see god, or hear him, not alone Moses, or certain prophets.] The *second* theory is intuition or mystical insight. Don't we all know how this never works? The *third* theory is based on "faith," which is blindly accepting someone else's having seen or felt god or having some mystical insight about him. The *fourth* theory depends on authority: (1) authority of an institution, the church or the state; (2) authority of a book, the Bible, the Koran, the Veda, the Upanishads; (3) authority of some individual prophet, or religious leader such as Moses, Christ, Mohammed, Lao-tse. The *fifth* theory set is based on so-called logical or rational proof, based on *a priori* grounds, or deductions from "self-evident truths."

Now these first four groups of arguments that I have listed here are not really seriously considered by any religious scholars (and I am talking about those who are against us). The religionists always get into the rational proofs; even the Roman Catholic church now uses them. They never fall back on direct sense experience, intuition, faith, or authority. They use rational arguments in our present scientific age.

Now many rational arguments have been proposed from time to time, but they may be reduced to variations of three main types. These have been given some fancy names; they are classified as the cosmological, the teleological, and the ontological arguments. Let's look at these jawbreakers for a moment.

The cosmological argument[8] is the most popular. This is based on the principle of cause, or the principle of "causality," holding that everything requires a cause to account for its existence. At first sight the argument appears convincing, but a very brief consideration reveals it offers no real proof. For the very same problem attaches to the supposed "first cause." This reminds me of a philosopher's (the philosopher was John Stuart Mill)[9] story concerning this particular argument. He was holding forth on the cosmological argument and had talked about it from time to time in his home until his little girl, age about six, came to him and said,

Daddy, you keep talking about god doing this and god causing things and god started the thing. I just want to ask you one question — who caused god?

That ended this theory, for if god "caused" everything, who created or caused god? If everything *must* have a cause, god himself had to have a cause to account for his existence; the first cause cannot be an "uncaused" cause. Another way to ask this question is "Who was god's mother?" at which point the cosmological argument becomes worthless theory.

Incidentally, when we talk of god everyone, including myself, keeps saying *he*. This reminds me of the joke which went around when Yury Gagarin[10] first flew around the world. It seems that a Southern newspaper correspondent interviewed him about his flight, and the correspondent asked Yury if he had seen god out in space. Gagarin said that no one had ever asked him this before. The Southern gentleman pressed for an answer. So Gagarin told him to brace himself and then he answered, "Yes, I saw god — and first of all, she is a Negro."

But to get back to who caused god, whether god is a she or a he and if she or he is Mongoloid, Negroid or Caucasian. In the cosmological argument, the theorist cannot solve his dilemma by postulating an uncaused first cause.

The second argument, the teleological argument, has as its general

---

[8]This argument was first advanced by Saint Thomas Aquinas (1224 or 1225–1274), Tommaso d'Aquino, Italian religious and philosopher.

[9]John Stuart Mill (1806–1873), son of James Mill, English philosopher and economist.

[10]Yury Alekseyevich Gagarin (1934–1968), Soviet cosmonaut and first man in space (1961).

thesis this wonderful word story: as we look at the world around us, we observe an order and a design[11] which makes the assumption of a planning intelligence unavoidable. Look at the stars; the moon comes up every night. Look at the plants, the seasons; there must have been a planning intelligence behind this. Well, the teleological view lies open to such easy attack that the modern theologians avoid it. What very little evidence there is of purpose in this world is overwhelmed by this conspicuous lack of *benevolent* purpose. The most unprejudiced mind can only allow that the universe appears indifferent to the life that swarms over it. Surely only an evil deity smiles on disease, earthquakes, defective children, floods, hurricanes, droughts, sickness, polio. The teleological argument is worthless.

The ontological argument is the chief hope of the theologians. Now, this holds that the existence of god is implied by his very nature. The concept of god is the concept of a perfect thing, and since we can formulate the concept of perfection it must be. Ah, come on now! Actually it is impossible to prove existence merely by the process of definition. For instance, if we decide to define or describe a little gnome, elf, leprechaun, or menahune in great detail, we cannot by the process of definition bring the gnome, elf, leprechaun, or menahune into actual existence. The ontological argument is worthless.

Recently two other arguments have been presented. One is the moral argument[12] that goodness, justice, truth, love, and wisdom flow from god. Since this leaves unsolved the problem of badness, injustice, untruth, hate, and folly, this argument fails. After all, if god is omnipotent, omniscient, omnipresent, and omnibenevolent, that is, all-powerful, all-knowing, everywhere present, and all good, how could he permit something evil? If he permits evil then he couldn't be all-powerful or all good, and this argument fails.

The second of the two most recent arguments is the pragmatic argument, and this asks us, "Does it work?" Is mankind advanced or retarded by faith in a god? Well, if history, with the crimes of the Inquisition, with the Crusades, with all the religious wars, if this does not answer

---

[11]Françoise-Marie Arouet, "Voltaire" (1694–1778), French writer. Voltaire's reply was that his nose, then, was especially designed by god so that his glasses could sit on it.
[12]See Kant's *Critique of Pure Reason* (Chicago: Encyclopaedia Britannica, Inc., 1952).

the question, we could demolish it by asking if a belief in Santa Claus would not do just as well.

Religion has caused more misery to all men in every stage of human history than any other single idea.

All right, you say, you don't like the arguments for god, but the Bible is still the greatest book in this world. It is good and it is true.

Well, I say, "Like hell it is." It is poor literature, poor history, and poor ethics. All in all, it has *nothing* to recommend it. The Bible is so unimportant that we hardly need to look at it.

I had not thought about it until I said it just then. It [the Bible] is so unimportant that few people even read it. Do you read it in your home? Most of the time people just accept for granted that the Bible is an important book. This isn't so.

Beginning in Genesis where there are two different stories of creation and going clear through the Old Testament one finds nothing but hatred, vengeance, cruelty, oppression, lust, deprivation. It is a perfectly horrible book. You don't need to take my word for it; just go and read it once. Can you honestly accept that story about Noah's Ark, or the Red Sea parting, or Eve being made out of Adam's rib, or the sun standing still, or Jonah and the whale? We all know that these were tall tales told in the age of ignorance and superstition, told at a time when men were fumbling for answers and when they did not have the resources and knowledge we have now.

The stories are pitiful. There is no beauty or love or understanding. Literally thousands of persons have written finer things, had better ideas. I would not trade one Madame Curie or one Einstein or one Lincoln for ten thousand Bible characters who could not sniff at the boots of the great men and women *who have labored for man.*

Ah, but you say again, that was the Old Testament — the New Testament is different. Oh, you can bet your life that it is — it's worse. You can yourself recount all the theories of when it was written, for they are multiple upon multiple — those theories. But casually glancing through it, the large problems of internal evidence are sufficient to discredit it. Why were there two genealogies of Christ, both quite different and traced through Joseph to prove his descent from David? *Joseph was not even his father.* The "holy ghost" was. Jesus did not descend from David. Why are there two versions of the Sermon on the Mount? Why can no one agree as to what Christ's last words were? When was he born?

16

Anyone who wants to argue the Bible can go ahead. It is not seriously considered anymore by any scholars of any intellectual repute. And if we did not have this Bible over which to argue, there would be the Koran or the Veda or the Torah. The thing we must do is simple: throw the whole thing out the window. God never wrote a book, simply because there is no god.

"How can you say that?" you ask. "Wouldn't it be better if you said you didn't know one way or the other? Why don't you admit that you are an agnostic?" Well, elementary, my dear Watson. Let me tell you in one word the difference between an Atheist and an agnostic. The difference is *guts*. I lose more agnostic friends by saying that. But let's go into detail again.

The term *agnostic* was coined by Sir Thomas Huxley in 1869. He designed a word which would indicate the exact opposite of gnosticism. Since the prefix "a" in words of Greek derivation ofttimes is a privative, that is, giving to the word a negative sense, he coined the word "agnostic" or agnosticism. He designed this word which would indicate the exact opposite of gnosticism. He was apparently studying gnosticism at the time.

Gnosticism was an eclectic system of philosophy and religion which flourished during the first six centuries of the present era. It sought to mediate between Christianity and paganism, from which Christianity was derived, and it taught that knowledge more than philosophy or more than faith was a means of salvation. According to this doctrine, all existences — both spiritual and material — originated in the deity by successive emanations or waves.

Well, here we are back again to the same question about which I talked before. Mind or matter, which came first? The gnostic solved the problem by proclaiming that each came in successive waves. First came mind and then came matter.

Then came mind and then came matter. These emanations or waves were called "eons," and Christ was conceived to be only a higher "eon" than ordinary man. One simple doctrine was that "emancipation," whatever that meant at that time to those poor serfs and peasants in Europe, came from "knowledge" or "gnosis." The possession of this gnosis saved the initiate from the dreadful clutch of matter. The "gnosis" or knowledge which they sought was so obscure (one great piece of knowledge was how many angels could dance on the point of a pin. The gnostics sought the answer, the "knowledge" about this, for years) that Huxley apparently was scoffing at it, and in scoffing at that he was scoffing at the type of knowledge which was present in Huxley's own day and is even present now. Let me read to you just a wee paragraph of "knowledge" from the gnostic's *Book of the Savior.*

Here we go; prepare yourself.

> And they that are worthy of the mysteries which lie in the ineffable are prior to the first mystery and also prior to the three statements which follow after them that all is my self. I am the treasure of man.[13]

Well, enough of that nonsense — that's knowledge?

So, technically, agnostics are those persons who do not believe in this kind of knowledge and who feel that it is relative and uncertain. They know that salvation will not come in this way. Huxley was more than a sarcastic wit. According to the Bible, when Paul visited Athens he admonished the people for a statue he found there. In Acts 17:23 he says,

> . . . as I passed by, and beheld your devotions, I found an altar with this inscription, TO THE UNKNOWN GOD.

Huxley thought, apparently, that god was as unknowable in 1869 as he had been in the time of Paul, and as Paul could well have done, Huxley coined a word for this phenomenon: God the great unknown.

But popularly, the word has been corrupted, probably deliberately corrupted as the words *Atheist* and *materialist* have been corrupted and by the same persons — the very powerful religionists. Popularly the word *agnostic* is felt to mean that the nature of god cannot be known *but that there is a god.* Therefore the agnostic is accepted in the community and he is accepted by the church. Agnosticism is very closely related to the religious doctrine that the ways of god are unfathomable, that human reason is fallible, and that man requires a different, non-scientific path to the truth. Agnostic philosophers, as distinguished from the man-on-the-street agnostics, are always allies of the church. The reason is that agnosticism, which puts forward the false notion that the world is unknowable, undermines science and reinforces theology. It

---

[13]G. R. S. Mead, *Pistis Sophia, a Gnostic Miscellany: Being for the Most Part Extracts from the Books of the Saviour,* reprint of the 1921 ed. (Secaucus, New Jersey: University Books, 1974.)

18

inclines man to faith, inducing him to trust religious doctrines. The test is always the same: does the church accept the existence of the creed? If it does, then the creed is not one which is in opposition to religion. The church does not anathematize the agnostic.

Thomas Huxley later wrote that he regretted coining the word because of the widespread misuse of the term by the public.

Well, that is what this Atheist is, and what I think. An A-theist is a materialist, a person who, simply, is *free from* theism (religion).

The second question I am always asked is "How did you get that way?" That is an exciting story too and the subject of my second speech, which will be given later this afternoon.

Thank you all for your attention.

The History of Materialism

Although many American Atheists do not like certain recent associations with the idea — the life-style of all Atheists is basically materialist.

There are all kinds of wrong ideas about materialism abroad in the land, perhaps purposely so, since this is a way of slandering the under-lying idea — to misinterpret it or to slur it.

There are, fundamentally, only two approaches to life. One is either a materialist or an idealist. I have spoken to this many times. From the beginning of mankind forward there were these two interpretations. The idealist viewpoint, which is championed these days as being that which has ideals, is very misunderstood generally, and substantively it is the basis of all religions. It should really be called "idea-ism" instead of ideal-ism because the basic premise of this philosophy is that idea was the first form, and all substantive things are expressions of idea. In the beginning was the big idea — god — an insubstantial director who created the material earth from his idea essence.

On the other hand there is materialism, which does not mean the love of material things. Materialism holds that nothing exists but natural phenomena, that there are no supernatural forces, nor can there be. Materialism attempts to find out the nature of nature — but does not presume to have the answers totally. We all find out as we go, don't we?

The question of the relationship of "idea" to "material things," i.e., nature, is the basic argument.

Those who regard nature as primary and thought as a property of nature (or a function of nature) belong to the camp of materialism.

Those who maintain that idea, or spirit, or mind existed before nature belong to the camp of idealism.

Materialism asserts that we think because we have a very physical brain which we use for thinking and that it can be measured in volume, in dimensions, and in weight as a physical thing. Idealism asserts that some ethereal big brain, somewhere, existed first and caused nature. In a way, the argument is academic since neither side knows with certainty where everything started, if it did start, or why, or when, but a kind of facing-of-life develops from the basic stance which one takes.

There have not been too many decent books written about the development of materialism, since no one really wants to touch it except to attack it. I have long looked for a book which might be impartial and doubt that any will be found because the basics in which the ideas are rooted cause too much subjective attachment to the one or the other. Unfortunately, the proponents of idealism have had possession of history writing, and teaching, in the Western world for sixteen hundred years, and this causes distortion and suppression of ideas.

With that preface, I have found a book from England printed in 1925. I had heard about the book from Atheist friends, but did not know too much about its contents. I was startled to see that it has an introduction written by Bertrand Russell. It would need to be good to have his endorsement. It is titled *The History of Materialism and Criticism of Its Present Importance.* The author is Frederick Albert Lange, professor of philosophy at the Universities of Zürich and Marburg. The book first appeared in 1865.[1] Lange himself was not a materialist. By and large, the attacks on the philosophy have been on ethical grounds. While he repeatedly stands against most of the forms of criticism on this ground, in the end he succumbs. Materialism is supposed to have a deleterious effect on conduct. Even today, when one is termed a materialist, the attack is that persons with this philosophy have a love for material things — that they are gluttons for rich living. It is incredible that such naïveté could continue to exist, but it does.

When Lange published his book in Germany, even the House of Huxley[2] in England suggested a translation of the book for that country. In 1874 it was the subject of much discussion when Professor Tyn-

---

[1] Frederick Albert Lange, *The History of Materialism and Criticism of Its Present Importance*, 3 vols. (London: Kegan Paul, Trench, Trubner & Co., Ltd., 1925).

22

dall[3] acknowledged his indebtedness "to the spirit and the letter" of the work. A translation was begun into English in 1875, but the author died in November of that year and the translator could not turn to him for assistance. The difficulties attending the translation of a philosophical German work into English are notorious. The man who translated the book was fundamentally an idealist, it appears from his introductory remarks. He has, he says, tried to translate literally as it was possible when working with the English (and the German) idiom.

This is an 1100-page book, and I am going to distill it. I am a materialist. I try to be honest and fair. This is the name of the game of materialism. But I have already decided that this is the best way to go when it comes to choosing a philosophy of life, so forgive me my trespasses in this matter if you perceive a bias of exultation as I proceed.

Most materialists despise philosophy and state that their views are in no way a product of philosophical speculation, but are the pure result of experience, of sound common sense, and of the physical sciences. Lange assumes that materialism is philosophy and that it had its roots with philosophy. Yet he notes that the beginning of consecutive thinking arose in the struggle against the traditional assumptions of religion. He states boldly, for a religious man,

> Religion has its roots in the earliest crudely inconsistent notions, which are ever being created afresh in indestructible strength by the ignorant masses.

The cosmogonies of the East, where life began, do not try to explain the world by means of a single principle, but offer anthropomorphic divinities, primal beings half sensuous, half spiritual — a chaotic reign of matter and forces in manifold changeful struggle and activity. In the presence of this mass of imaginative ideas, awakening thought calls for order and unity — and thus was philosophy born as a call for order and unity.

---

[2]House of Huxley refers to the prestigious English family of letters and science: Thomas Henry Huxley (1825–1895), English biologist; Sir Julian Sorell Huxley (1887–1975), grandson of T. H., English biologist; Aldous Leonard (1894–1963), brother of Julian, English novelist and critic; Andrew Fielding Huxley (1917–), British physiologist and educator.
[3]John Tyndall (1820–1893), British physicist.

Looking at this, Lange begins with certain assumptions (remember that he is writing over one hundred years ago) that

Materialism only becomes a complete system when matter is conceived as purely material; that is, when its constituent particles are not a sort of thinking matter, but physical bodies, which are moved in obedience to merely physical principles, and being themselves without sensations, produce sensation, and thought by particular forms of their combinations.

Materialists of the Atheist school feel that these physical bodies, which move in obedience to physical principles (and we don't say "merely" physical principles — they are not "merely"; they are all that is), do produce sensations and even ideas. We could not feel pain without nerves and nerve endings. We could not have ideas without brains. The space between us — my sitting here and all of you out there — that space between us will never create love itself, but a very physical human being can love, manifesting that love through a physical body and a physical brain.

We always hark back to Greece and Rome. It may be because our current religious heritage developed in a straight line from that culture. But in Greece, to start there, we must remember that there was the aristocracy and the mass of people. What the mass believed the aristocracy shunned, and what the aristocracy believed and promulgated was not accessible to the mass. We must also remember that the Greeks had no political unity in which a complete religion could be developed. There were individual city-states. There were many local interpretations of their cults. Today in America we have the same: the Baptists dominate the South, the Mormons are supreme in Utah, the big cities belong to the Roman Catholics. Yet there is some intercourse between us all — and the grounds on which we all meet are benign, stripped of any particular regional or religious emphasis, *usually*. When we watch a national television show, it must be palatable to all. No one dare be offended, and so we continue to cater to "Western dramas," "mystery and detective tales," and other areas in which there can be no major philosophical confrontation.

Athens was peculiar. It was there that Sokrates[4] had to drink the hemlock. It was from thence that Aristotle[5] fled, as did Protagoras.[6] The works of the latter, on the gods, were publicly burned. Anaxagoras[7] was arrested there and obliged to flee. Theodorus, called "the Atheist"[8] [who is not listed in any contemporary encyclopedias or biographical

24

dictionaries], and Diogenes of Apollonia[9] were prosecuted as deniers of the gods. All of this happened in humane and enlightened Athens.

This dawn of scientific speculation in Greece, which Lange calls philosophy, began, however, at a time when there was a great religious movement in the East. It is even possible that with the travel of that time the philosophical ideas came from the East to Greece and were developed there because suitable intellectual circumstances had been prepared by the Greeks' own development.

However, the thinkers were persecuted — in Athens, at least. There was in Greece, apparently, no priestly caste, but there were priestly families whose hereditary rights were preserved with the most inviolable legitimism, and to which, as a rule, belonged the highest aristocracy — maintaining their rule for centuries. These persons had in their possession the "Eleusinian mysteries."[10] The great families were the Eumolpidae, the Kerykes, the Phyllidae and, in the matter of the attack on Diagoras of Melos,[11] who had come to Athens to propound, we see that

---

[4]Sokrates (ca. 470–399 B.C.), Greek philosopher who developed the Sokratic method of inquiry and instruction, consisting of a series of questions designed to elicit a clear expression of something supposed to be implicitly known by rational beings.

[5]Aristotle (384–322 B.C.), Greek philosopher who wrote on logic, metaphysics, natural science, ethics, politics, rhetoric, and poetics.

[6]Protagoras (485–410 B.C.), Greek philosopher and first of the sophists. His philosophy is epitomized in the famous saying, "Man is the measure of all things."

[7]Anaxagoras (ca. 520–ca. 458 B.C.), Greek philosopher who first introduced the dualistic explanation of the universe.

[8]Theodorus was born in Cyrene in 320 B.C. and was a pupil of Arete, the daughter of Aristippos, who had been a pupil of Sokrates. Details of his life are preserved in book ii, chapters viii and xii, of Diogenes Laertius, *Peri biōn dogmatōn kai apophthegmatōn tōn en philosophia eudokimēsantōn* ("Lives, Teachings, and Sayings of Famous Philosophers"), volumes 184 and 185 of the Loeb Classical Library, published by Harvard University Press.

[9]Diogenes of Apollonia (fifth century B.C.), Greek philosopher, promulgated cosmology in which air was the source of being.

[10]Eleusinian mysteries: concerned with the abode of the blessed after death.

the family of Eumolpidae was authorized, under certain circumstances, to pass judgment against religious offenders according to a secret code whose author was entirely unknown. There was, as now, power vested in established religious fanaticism, from whence came religious (and political) assault against those who would not conform.

Aristophanes[12] and Epikuros[13] participated in all the external religious ceremonies and could thus escape with jesting or bitter mockery as long as compliance with existing form was shown. That sounds like modern America. From the standpoint of the multitude, every thinker — even the most ideal — must be prosecuted as a denier of the gods, for no thinker pictures the gods as the priestly tradition describes them to the masses.

It was in the circle of men who were wealthy, distinguished, and had a wide experience gained from travel, that philosophy arose. Thales,[14] Herakleitos,[15] Empedokles,[16] Anaximander[17] had such prominent positions that it is not to be wondered at that they were not brought to account for their opinions. Who would question the esoteric writings of a Rockefeller, or a Ford, or a Mellon, or a Firestone? Indeed, who among the masses would even know what those persons were writing? It was about the same in Greece.

---

[11]Diagoras of Melos (fifth century B.C.), called "the Atheist," Greek sophist and poet.

[12]Aristophanes (ca. 450–ca. 388 B.C.), Athenian playwright, regarded as one of the greatest writers of comedies of all times.

[13]Epikuros (341–270 B.C.), Greek philosopher who emphasized that pleasure is the only good and the end of morality.

[14]Thales (625?–?547 B.C.), Greek philosopher and scientist, discovered the five geometric theorems. Known as the father of Greek philosophy, he predicted an eclipse of the sun for May 28, 585 B.C..

[15]Heracleitos (ca. 540–ca. 480 B.C.), Greek philosopher, evolved cosmology in which fire is principal element of all things.

[16]Empedokles (ca. 490–430 B.C.), Greek philosopher and statesman, developed theory of four elements to compose physical world; founder of rhetoric.

[17]Anaximander (610–ca. 547 B.C.), Greek astronomer and philosopher, taught that primary substance is eternal and indestructible matter; discovered obliquity of the ecliptic; introduced the sundial; and invented geographical maps.

But hand in hand with the intellectual movement called philosophy, there was the study of mathematics and natural science. Thales, Anaximander, and Anaximenes[18] busied themselves with special problems of astronomy, and with an explanation of the universe. Commerce was causing knowledge to flow in all directions. In the East the scholars were much ahead of Greece in mathematics and in astronomy.

In the study — the beginning study — of these sciences, and in the beginning freeing of minds from the mist of wonder, in transferring the study of the world from the dazzling fable-land of religious and poetical ideas to the sphere of reason and sober theory, it was necessary to start with materialism.

External physical things are everywhere. The "Atomists" broke through. Amongst all the properties of things, they assigned to matter only the simplest and attempted then to develop from these the whole aggregate of phenomena.

The Atomists supplied the first perfectly clear conception of what is to be understood as "matter," the substratum of all phenomena. This step, says Lange, "was as bold and courageous as it was methodically correct . . . for so long as men started at all . . . this was the only way of explaining. . . ." They progressed from the simple to explain the complex and from the known to explain the unknown, instead of attempting to explain the other way round, which had basically been the religious approach.

Demokritos

Yet, and quoting Lange now, "With few great men of antiquity can history have dealt so despitefully as with Demokritos."[19] In the distorted picture of unscientific tradition almost nothing appears of him except the name of the "laughing philosopher." So, Lange notes that he admires the tact with which Bacon[20] — ordinarily no great hero of historical learning — chose exactly Demokritos out of all the philosophers of antiquity and awarded him the premium for true investigation — while

---

[18]Anaximenes (ca. 380–ca. 280), Greek rhetorician and historian, accompanied Alexander the Great to Persia.

[19]Lange's spelling will be used on all names in this essay.

[20]Francis Bacon, 1st Baron Verulam and Viscount St. Albans (1561–1626), English philosopher and author.

he considers Aristotle the originator of an injurious appearance of knowledge (falsely called) and of an empty philosophy of words.

Actually, Atomism is the basis, the foundation of modern natural science and if father there is of it — Demokritos must be that.

He was described in Webster's *Dictionary* as a Greek philosopher who lived about 460 B.C.[21] and who was popularly known as "The Laughing Philosopher."

Demokritos was a citizen of the Ionian colony of Abdera on the Thracian coast. The prosperous commercial city was wealthy and cultivated. Demokritos' father was a man of unusual wealth. There is scarcely room to doubt that the highly gifted son enjoyed an excellent education, but there is no historical foundation for the story that he was brought up by Persian magi. That story was probably composed because of the visit of Xerxes I[22] to the city of Abdera. There is no doubt that the king had with him his most learned magi. Also, it would be obvious that when such a person visited a town such as Abdera, the king and his court would be housed with one of the richest and most influential citizens. Demokritos' father was such a man.

Actually there has been much research as to the possible age of Demokritos. It is not known if he was a contemporary of Sokrates or not. At all events, Demokritos only began to develop his doctrines when he had reached a mature age, and it is possible that he lived at about the same time.

Demokritos appears to have spent his whole patrimony in the "grand tour" — visiting all existing cities, acquainting himself with the countries and the cultures of his time. Returning to his home in poverty, he was supported by his brother but soon, by his successful predictions in the sphere of natural philosophy, he gained the reputation of being a wise and heaven-inspired man. Finally, he wrote his great work *Dialosmos*. With the public reading of this, he was rewarded by his native city with a gift of one hundred (according to some, five hundred) talents (the unit of money) and with the erection of commemorative statues.

The year of Demokritos' death is uncertain, but there is a general admission that he reached a very advanced age, and died cheerfully and painlessly.

A great number of sayings and anecdotes are connected with his

---

[21]Demokritos in 1990 was given as *ca.* 460–*ca.* 370 B.C.
[22]Xerxes I (*ca.* 519–465 B.C.), the Great King of Persia (486–465 B.C.).

name, though the greater portion of them have no particular import for the character of the man to whom they relate. This is especially so of the interpretation which has been put upon him as "The Laughing Philosopher," which makes the historians see in him nothing but a merry jester over the follies of the world, and a holder of a philosophy which (without losing itself in profundities) regards everything from the good side. Amid all the contradictory stories we find that he did devote his whole life to scientific investigations, which were as serious and logical as they were extensive.

The primary collectors of the scattered fragments, which are all that remain to us of his numerous works, regard him as occupying the first place for genius and knowledge amongst all the philosophers before Aristotle. It is very significant that a man of such extensive attainments would have a fragment of his thought remaining which says, "we should strive not after fullness of knowledge, but fullness of understanding." When he speaks of his achievements, he dwells not upon the number and variety of his writings, but of his personal observation, his mathematical method and his intercourse with other learned men. He notes:

> Amongst all my contemporaries, I have traveled over the largest portion of the earth in search of things the most remote, and have seen the most climate and countries, heard the largest number of thinkers, and no one has excelled me in geometric construction and demonstration — not even the geometers of the Egyptians, with whom I spent five years as a guest.

One of the circumstances which caused Demokritos to fall into oblivion was his want of ambition and his distaste for dialectic discussion. He is said to have been in Athens without making himself known to one of its philosophers. Amongst his moral aphorisms we find the following: "He who is fond of contradiction and makes many words is incapable of learning anything that is right."

Demokritos founded no school. His words were copied from, and his whole philosophy was finally absorbed by Epikuros. Aristotle mentions him frequently with respect. However, he cites him only when he attacks him, and this is not done with fairness or objectivity, albeit with respect. Yet we know much about Demokritos, mostly because of his clearness and consecutiveness in thinking. We may consider the following propositions as the essential foundations of his teaching.

I. Out of nothing arises nothing; nothing that is can be de-

stroyed. *All change is only combination and separation of atoms.*

This proposition contains in principle the two great doctrines of modern physics — the theory of the indestructibility of matter and that of the persistence of force (or conservation of energy). This stands, of course, in contradiction to the Christian concept of creation, "out of nothing arises everything."

Essentially from this proposition came the theory of the universe which we use today in physics and astronomy.

II. Nothing happens by chance, but everything through a cause and of necessity.

When a tile falls upon a man's head while he is walking down the street, this is regarded as an accident. Yet no one doubts the direction of the wind, the law of gravitation, and other natural circumstances, which fully determined the event, so that it followed from a physical necessity that, in fact, any head which appeared there at that particular moment would be struck by a tile.

Although there may be an assumption of chance error, there were numbers of causes involved.

III. Nothing exists but atoms and empty space; all else is only opinion.

On this atomic theory we explain today the laws of sound, of light, of heat, of chemical and physical changes.

IV. The atoms are infinite in number, and of endless variety of form. In the eternal fall through infinite space, the greater, which fall more quickly, strike against the lesser, and later movements and vortices that thus arise are the commencement of the formation of worlds. Innumerable worlds are formed and perish successively and simultaneously.

Later, Epikuros comes to the simple conclusion that in empty space there is no resistance; all bodies must fall equally fast.

V. The variety of all things is a consequence of the variety of their atoms in number, size, figure, and arrangement; there is no qualitative difference of atoms. They have no "internal conditions" and act on each other only by pressure or collision.

30

Demokritos regarded the sense qualities such as color, sound, heat, and so on as mere appearances. He felt that these were caused by the arranging of the atoms in a schema or schemata.

> VI. The soul [defined as the essence of life — ed.] consists of fine, smooth, round atoms, like those of fire. These atoms are the most mobile, and by their motion, which permeates the whole body, the phenomena of life are produced.

He conceived of the intellect as "a phenomenon taking its origin from the mathematical constitution of certain atoms in their relation to the others."

From these propositions, he derived ethical concepts, which briefly stated are that:

> Happiness consists in the cheerful calmness of spirit which man can attain only by securing the mastery over his desires. Temperance and purity of heart, united with culture of the emotions and development of the intelligence, supply every man with the means, despite the vicissitudes of life, of reaching this goal. Sensual pleasure affords only a brief satisfaction; and he only who does good for the sake of its intrinsic merit, without being swayed by fear or hope is sure of this inward reward.

Demokritos was aware of how organic bodies adapted to environmental situations and considered the human frame to be especially so adapted. His view of the world was objective, not subjective.

Had Western civilization proceeded from this point and built upon it, we could have eliminated the thousand years of the "Dark Ages" which prevailed in Europe after the ascendancy of Christianity. But let us follow the thread and see how materialism moved after these original propositions were given to the world. The philosophy flowered again only in recent times, but perhaps we can see what subverted it.

Demokritos wrote seventy books and Plato[23] wished to burn all of them. Two of these books were on psychology, one on the mind and the other on the senses. He taught that the seat of the mind was the brain and he called it "the monarch of the body."

---

[23]Plato, original name Aristocles (ca. 428–348 [or 347] B.C.), Greek philosopher, laid philosophical foundations of Western culture.

In late antiquity there is a story that the sage once saw a porter in his native town packing together in a very ingenious manner the wood blocks he had to carry. He talked to him and was so surprised by his quickness that he took him as a pupil. This man was supposed to have been Protagoras, the first of the Sophists.

Demokritos was a happy man, which is the condition of most materialists. He felt that the distinctions of good and evil, right and wrong are to be known instinctively without inquiry. He found cheerful serenity of soul to be the most lasting good, but that it could be attained most readily through right thinking and acting, as a result of experience. The reason for striving after this harmonious inward condition is reason enough for the happiness of the individual.

And we Atheists think he was right and that we are right.

The history of materialism is a neglected subject matter because of the contempt which has been poured upon this philosophy by the theistic historians. It is only recently that it has been able to crop out again in the intellectual community. From whence came the philosophy of materialism and why has been obscured by historians and philosophers. It is difficult, as Lange found, to search through the morass for a clean line and bring that to you.

A long series of men were traveling through the cities of Greece, teaching and disputing, and in some cases making great fortunes doing so. The cleverest youths (of rich families naturally) flocked to them to partake of their instructions, and this became the mark of fashion. Their doctrines and their speeches became the daily topics of the upper classes, and their fame spread with incredible rapidity.

Protagoras

Protagoras, who is next to be considered, was the first to start not from an objective viewpoint, but from the subjective viewpoint of the spirit of man. Protagoras dropped the Atomism, that everything was composed of atoms, which had been proposed by Demokritos. He regarded matter as what it appears to the individual. He called this Sensationalism, meaning that it was the sensation or feeling to the individual observing which counted most.

His propositions, underlying this Sensationalism, were:

(1) Man is the measure of all things: of those that are that they are; of those that are not that they are not.
(2) Contradictory assertions are equally true.

Lange interprets this as follows:

Man is the measure of things, that is, it depends upon our sensations how things appear to us, and this appearance is all that is given us; and it is not man in his universal and necessary qualities, but each individual in each single moment, that is the measure of things.

However, the individual is mutable. If the same temperature appears to the same man at one time cool, at another warm, both impressions are in their own moment equally true, and there is no truth outside of this.

From this, Protagoras moved to explain desire and perception as the principle of action. He drew a sharp distinction with a good citizen and noble man who desires only for what is good and noble and the bad and vulgar who feel attracted toward evil. But in his unconditioned relativity, he must have seen that the right and good for the man in each case would be what seems to that man to be right and good. The person attracted to evil perceives it as right and good.

From this Lange extrapolates in his thinking so that Ethical Materialism is perceived to be an end result of Protagoras' idea. He defines Ethical Materialism as a moral doctrine which makes the moral action of man rise from the particular emotions of his spirit, which determines the object of action by the effort after a desired condition — happiness. He argues that such an ethical system must be materialistic because it starts from matter — the elementary matter of practical conduct, the impulses, the feelings of pleasure and its opposite — and hence, materialism is ignoble. But this is Lange's interpretation.

Protagoras was driven from Athens for having begun his book on the gods with the words, "As to the gods, I do not know whether they exist or not."

So long as a state, or a city-state, in the case of Athens, steadily develops and holds fast to old traditions, all its citizens feel themselves held together by a common interest as against other states. A thinker embraces in a short series of conclusions results which history requires thousands of years to realize. Although the idea may be quite right, yet in a particular case it may be prejudicial because it destroys the interest of the citizens in their country, and in consequence cripples the country's vital force. So long as men adhere to their traditions, there are certain ultimate limits set to the ambition and the talents of the individual. All these limits are removed by the principle that each individual man has in himself the measure of all things. The only security against this is the merely conventional — and Protagoras was in difficulties.

When Protagoras tried to establish that contradictory assertions are equally true, many of his imitators cared only to establish their own personal views.

In addition, Protagoras busied himself with the rudiments of grammatical and etymological studies — that is, the study of words. He finally came around to the proposition that "all is number," that "soul in essence is number" and that "god is number."

From all of this derived a certain school called that of the Sophists. There was a boundlessness of their relativity, their vague acceptance of the middle-class morality without the establishment of any principle, the pliant individualism which everywhere assumes to itself the right to throw down or let stand as suits the purpose of the moment.

The school went on to distinguish later Sophists merely by a confident insistence upon the principle of subjectivity or individual will.

It was as a reaction to this that the school of idealism began to flourish. In Plato and Aristotle it secured a decided victory. Yet what they defeated was not materialism but an aberration from it.

History has frequently shown that if the educated men begin to laugh at the gods, or to resolve their existence into philosophical abstractions, immediately the half-educated masses, becoming unsteady and unquiet, seize upon every folly in order to exalt it into a religion.

Asiatic cults with fantastic practices found favor. The pre-elements of Christianity began to coalesce and we were on our way then to intellectual stultification.

Materialism had given preference to the mathematical and physical investigations. With Protagoras it reached its dissolution — an entirely new foundation was required. There was not a straight-line development, for philosophizing men interceded in the natural outreaching development of the ideas of materialism, Protagoras being one of these.

Sokrates

Ideas which are too advanced for one age must die there and then invigorate themselves once more by a struggle with reaction before they painfully and again struggle to the front. Sokrates called to life the new tendency to reaction. Athens was a pious city and Sokrates was a genuine Athenian. His theory of the world was a distinctly religious one — the teleological conception of nature — of gods creating and working in human fashion. He renounced speculation as to the essence of things and instead made the moral nature of man the supreme object of his philosophy.

His conviction was that the reason which had created the world-structure proceeded after the manner of human reason. The world, to him, is explained from man, not man from the universal laws of nature. In everything he put forth there was anthropomorphic activity. A plan, a purpose, must first be provided, and then the matter and the force to set it going. The architect of the worlds must be a person who can be conceived and imagined by man, though he may not be understood in all his actions. If this man, this being, is equated with reason, the words *reason* and *god* can be employed as convertible terms, and Sokrates can scarcely speak with sufficient contempt of "the search after external causes."

Sokrates was not alone content to maintain the ordinary form of religious cultus, but imparted to all a deeper meaning. Thus, he demanded that the people not pray for particular blessings, but rather require "good" from the gods, since they best know what is good for us. But Hellenic prayer was bound up with the existence of particular gods. Each god then became the representative of a purer creed. Sokrates also praised the oracles — for a god who has taken thought in the smallest details for the good of man must also hold intercourse with man and counsel him.

This spiritual movement, inaugurated by Sokrates, underwent various modifications in the systems of Plato and Aristotle, whose works dominated the minds of civilized man in the Western world for over a thousand years. Yet the absurd teachings of Aristotle are glossed over even today. He taught that the universe was a closed sphere, in the center of which he fixed the earth. He held that a vacuum could not exist. He taught that fleas and lice were produced out of dust. He taught that only man had the beating of the heart; that the left side of the body was colder than the right; that man had more teeth than woman; that there is an empty space at the back of every man's head; that heavy bodies fall faster than light ones.

Lange explains it thus:

A tendency, after spreading vigorously and completely permeating a whole epoch, begins to die out, and loses its hold upon new generations. Meanwhile fresh forces arise from other, and hitherto invisibly, working currents of thought, and adapting themselves to the changed character of the nations and states, issue a new

35

watchword. A generation exhausts itself in the production of ideas, like the soil which produces the same crop too long; and the richest harvest always springs from the fallow fields.

I can't accept that. Materialism was thoroughly suppressed by violent forms as often as not. Idealism was promoted with the sword, and with the support of civic governments whom it served. It was only as it came to a shambles that it could be rechallenged by the suppressed materialism being sought out again.

As we try to seek out its history, we find that the difficulty is that everyone who ever wrote on materialism has been so biased against it that there is almost no chance at all to find out what the actual history of it was, who was really involved, and what those persons really had to say. Lange's intrusive remarks confirm this.

Epikuros is one of our primitive materialists. His father was said to have been a poor schoolmaster of Athens who became a colonist at Samos. There, Epikuros was born toward the end of the year 342 B.C., or at the beginning of 341. In his fourteenth year, the story is given that he was studying Hesiod's[24] Cosmogony at school and finding that everything was explained to arise from chaos, he cried out and asked, "Whence, then, came chaos?" When his teacher had no reply, young Epikuros began to philosophize for himself.

Indeed, he was self-taught. The most important ideas which he incorporated in his system were — individually — already known. His general education is said to have been deficient. He joined himself to none of the then prevailing schools, but studied the writings of Demokritos.

Greece was in a state of decline. Alexander the Great[25] had died suddenly at Babylon and freedom was being suppressed by Antipater.[26] Amidst the confusion, Epikuros taught in different cities, only returning to Athens in the maturity of his years. He never filled any public office. He never came into conflict with religion. He sedulously honored the gods with all conventional observances, without pretending to a belief concerning them which he did not really feel.

Of death, he said:

---

[24]Hesiod (eighth century B.C.), Greek poet; an earlier work, Theogony, was an account of the beginnings of the world and birth of the gods.
[25]Alexander III, the Great (356–323 B.C.), king of Persia (336–323).
[26]Antipater (ca. 397–ca. 319 B.C.), Macedonian general.

That so long as we are, there is as yet no death; but as soon as death comes, then we exist no more. Our fear of death is not caused by our dread of non-existence; what makes us regard it with such terror is the fact that we involuntarily combine with the idea of nothingness an idea of life, that is, the notion of feeling this nothingness. We imagine that a dead man is conscious, that the soul continues to exist and to feel. If only we could succeed in wholly separating the idea of life from its opposite, and bravely relinquish all thought of immortality, death would lose its terrors. We should say to ourselves: death is not an evil; neither for him who is dead, for he has no feeling; nor for the living, for him death does not yet exist. As long as we are alive, death does not exist for us, and when death appears we no longer exist. Hence we can never come in contact with death; we never feel its icy touch, which we dread so much.

Epikuros wrote three hundred books, but the believers in gods saw to it that not one was preserved. Only fragments quoted by other authors remain. According to Epikuros, the great evil that afflicts mankind is fear: fear of the gods and fear of death. To get rid of these fears was the ultimate aim of his ethics. He believed in making science to be the servant of life.

Epikuros taught the atomic theory of Demokritos. He held that matter was the positive principle of all things, in opposition to Plato's teaching that matter is nonbeing. Epikuros held that matter is composed of innumerable uncreated and indestructible atoms in perpetual motion. The creation or destruction of the world was out of the question. Atoms, space and weight, that is, mechanical causes, were sufficient to explain the world, and he scoffed at the idea of final causes.

He taught that the laws of nature were to be discovered by actual observation of facts. To abandon observation is to depart from facts and to land in the region of idle fantasies. He taught that the moon might get its light from the sun. He also believed in explaining things in household words instead of confounding ideas by strange sounding technical terminology. He rejected the Greek dialectics. His own logic was distinctly sensorial and empirical.

All the virtues are derived by Epikuros from wisdom, which teaches us that man cannot be happy unless he is wise, noble, and just; and, conversely, that man cannot be wise, noble, and just without being really happy. Thus, the whole object of the explanation of nature is to free us from fear and anxiety.

In his maturity, when he returned to Athens, he bought a garden there, where he dwelt with his disciples. It is said to have borne as an inscription, "Stranger, here will it be well with thee: here pleasure is the highest good." He lived with his fellows temperately and simply, in harmonious effort, in heartfelt friendship, as a united family. In his will he bequeathed the garden to his school, which for a long time still had its center there.

According to Epikuros the ultimate basis of all knowledge is sensible perception. This in itself is always true; only through its relation to an object does an error arise. If a madman sees a dragon, this perception, as such, is not deceptive — he does perceive the picture of a dragon, and no reason and no law of thought can alter the fact. But if he believes that this dragon he "sees" will devour him, there he is wrong. The error lies in the referring of the perception to an objective fact. It is an error of the same kind as when a scientific man, after the most sober inquiry, incorrectly explains some celestial phenomenon. The perception is true; the reference to an assumed cause is false.

Thus, with regard to the moon, Epikuros supposed that it might have its own light, but its light might also come from the sun. If it is suddenly eclipsed it may be that there is a temporary extinction of the light; it may also be that the earth has interposed between the sun and moon, and so by its shadow caused the eclipse. You may choose which view you prefer — only let your explanation remain a natural one. This natural explanation must rest upon analogy with other known cases. The right study of nature must not arbitrarily propose new laws, but must everywhere base itself upon actually observed facts. So soon as we abandon the way of observation, we have lost the traces of nature and are straying into the region of idle fantasies.

It appears incredible today that this could have been proposed three hundred years before Christ and that we could have so long lost our way.

Epikuros went further. He recognized the formation of memory-pictures, which arise from repeated perception, and which, therefore, as compared with the individual perception, have already the character of a universal. This universal, or what is equivalent to a universal idea, is less certain than the original individual idea, but can at the same time, just because of its universal nature, play a much greater part in thought. For example, one sees a number of individual horses and finally has the idea of "horse" as an idea apart from the individual horses one has seen.

The criterion of the truth of all universals is always their ratification by perception, which is the basis of all knowledge. The universals are not, therefore, by any means especially certain or true. They are, primarily, only "opinions" which are spontaneously developed out of the contact of man with things. These opinions are true if they are ratified by perceptions.

Epikuros was the most fertile writer amongst the ancients. He used radical sense by radical meaning to get to the root. This is not infrequently united with materialistic views — a disdain for the historical, as compared with the scientific, element.

Epikuros was hated for three reasons: 1) he was self-taught and attached himself to none of the dominant schools; 2) he hated dialectic and employed a universally intelligible mode of speech; 3) he never quoted, and as a rule simply ignored, those who thought differently from himself.

Yet Lange summarizes his teachings on nature as follows (to give you an idea of how far advanced he was):

Out of nothing, nothing comes, for otherwise anything could come out of nothing. Everything that is is body; the only thing that is not body is empty space.

Among bodies some are formed by combination; the others are those out of which all combinations are formed. These are indivisible and absolutely immutable. The universe is unbounded and therefore the number of bodies must also be endless.

The atoms are in constant motion, in part widely removed from each other, while in part they approach each other and combine. But of this there was never a beginning. The atoms have no qualities except size, figure, and weight.

Similarly the time in which the atoms move in the void is quite inexpressibly short; their movement is absolutely without hindrance. The figures of the atoms are of inexpressible variety, and yet the number of actually recurring forms is not absolutely infinite, because in that case the formations possible in the universe could not be confined within definite, even though extremely wide limits.

In a finite body the number as well as the variety of the atoms is limited, and therefore there is no such thing as infinite divisibility. In void space there is no above or below; and yet even here one direction of motion must be opposed to another. Such directions are innumerable, and with regard to them we can, in thought, imagine above and below.

We, of course, today, with refinements, premise our understanding of the world and nature upon the idea of atoms.

But in his *Last Words on Materialism*, Prof. Ludwig Büchner[27] says:

> Epicurus brings the history of ancient materialism to a close, which now for fifteen centuries or more passes almost entirely into oblivion through the overwhelming influence of Christianity. Only timidly and under deceptive disguises materialism dared, after the expiration of this time, to show itself again in a few philosophical thinkers of the Middle Ages such as Petrus Pomponatius,[28] Giordano Bruno,[29] Gassendi[30] and others, some of whom had to atone for their doctrines on the funeral pyre.

Among all the peoples of antiquity, none perhaps was by nature further removed than were the Romans from materialistic views. Their religion had its roots deep in superstition; their whole political life was circumscribed by superstitious forms. They clung with peculiar tenacity to the sentiments they inherited; art and science had little charm for them, and they were still less inclined to bury themselves in the contemplation of nature.

For centuries after their first contact with the Greeks there continued that antipathy to any scientific studies. It was only after the defeat of Hannibal[31] that Greek art and literature gradually forced their way into Rome. Schools of Greek philosophy and rhetoric were opened and frequently again forbidden.

However, this could not remain, and by the last days of the Republic,

---

[27]Ludwig Büchner (1824–1899), German physician and philosopher, *Last Words on Materialism and Kindred Subjects* (London: Watts & Co., 1901).

[28]Pietro Pomponazzi (1462–1525), Italian philosopher, whose *De Immortalitate Animi* (1516) argued that the soul was mortal.

[29]Giordano Bruno, originally Filippo (1548–1600), Italian philosopher, critic of Aristotelian logic, and champion of Copernican cosmology.

[30]Pierre Gassendi (1592–1655), French philosopher, who revived the system of Epikuros and opposed it to that of Aristotle, in his *Exercitationes Paradoxicae adversus Aristoteleos* (1624, 1654).

[31]Hannibal (247–183 B.C.), Cathaginian general who waged war against Rome.

every educated Roman understood Greek and the young nobles pursued their studies in Greece. Of all the schools of Greek philosophy there were two which especially captivated the Romans — the Stoic and the Epikurean. The first, with its blunt pride in virtue, related to the Roman character. The mass of men regarded an Epikurean as a slave of his lusts (not understanding the materialist base of his philosophy). Cicero, unfortunately, popularized the Epikurean doctrine in this sense of the word.

Titus Lucretius

The theory of Epikuros was in every way purer and nobler than the practice of these Romans. Two courses, thus, were open to them. The Romans either allowed themselves to be purified and become modest and temperate, or they could corrupt the theory. Virgil[32] did this, as did Horace.[33] But among the Roman semi-philosophers there was a thorough and genuine Epikurean, Titus Lucretius.[34] His didactic poem *De Rerum Natura* contributed more than anything else in Rome, when learning revived, to resuscitate the doctrines of Epikuros and to set them in a more favorable light.

Of the life of Titus Lucretius Carus scarcely anything is known. It appears that amidst the confusion of the civil war, he sought some stability for his inner life, and found it in the philosophy of Epikuros. His great poem was undertaken to make a convert to this school of his friend, the poet Memmius.

Apparently the thing which attracted Lucretius to Epikuros and inspired him with this eager enthusiasm shown in his poem was the boldness and moral vigor with which Epikuros robbed the theistic beliefs of their sting, in order to base morality upon an impregnable foundation of nature. This is shown clearly enough by Lucretius, for immediately after the splendid poetical introduction to Memmius, he goes on:

> When human life to view lay foully prostrate upon earth, crushed down under the weight of religion, who showed her head

---

[32]Publius Virgilius Maro (70–19 B.C.), Roman poet.
[33]Quintus Horatius Flaccus (65–8 B.C.), Roman poet and satirist.
[34]Titus Lucretius Carus (*ca.* 96–*ca.* 55 B.C.), Roman poet and philosopher.

from the quarters of heaven with hideous aspect lowering upon mortals, a man of Greece ventured first to lift up his mortal eyes to her face, and first to withstand her to her face. Him neither story of gods, nor thunderbolts, nor heaven with threatening roar, could quell, but only stirred up the more — the eager courage of his soul filling him with desire to be the first to burst the fast bars of Nature's portals.

We do know this about Epikuros — but we do not know what was contained in the over three hundred books which he wrote. Lucretius had recourse to many additional sources which we do not have. He industriously studied Empedokles. Lucretius had a strong moral character and could afford sublime sentiments in his poem. He displayed purity, vigor, and force of comprehension which were rare at the time and perhaps have not been met with from the days of Lucretius to our own.

Yet the introduction to the poem consists of an invocation to the goddess Venus,[35] which is immediately afterward, as I have just quoted, attacked. He shows that religion, which once cruelly oppressed mankind, had been thrown down and trodden underfoot, and he raises the question whether this philosophy, which has thus overthrown religion, may not lead us into the paths of immorality and sin.

He shows how, on the contrary, religion is the source of the grossest abominations and how it is this unreasonable terror of eternal punishment which leads mankind to sacrifice their happiness and peace of mind to the horrors of the prophets.

He then develops the materialist theme that nothing can ever come from nothing. Similarly it is shown that nothing, again, is really destroyed, but that the particles of perishing things are dispersed, just as they had come together, in order to constitute the thing. Then, in the poem, follows the proof that the universe is not filled with matter, that it is, rather, a void space in which the atoms move. There is nothing besides the atoms and void. All existing things are either combinations of these two or an "event" of these. Even time has no separate existence, but is the feeling of a succession of occurrences earlier and later. The events of history are to be regarded only as accidents of bodies and of space. All bodies are either simple atoms or are compounds of atoms.

---

[35]The Roman goddess of love and beauty.

If simple atoms, they cannot be destroyed because there are limits to the divisibility of matter so that things are preserved.

At the conclusion of the first book, Lucretius discusses the constitution of the universe. He declines, above all things, to admit definite limits to the world. It is extraordinarily interesting to any thoughtful observer, how difficult it was, and is, to attain a correct theory of nature — as we see in this ancient Roman try.

After positing these premises, he proposes (from Empedokles) that all the adaptation to be found in the universe, and especially in organic life, is merely a special case of the infinite possibilities of mechanical events. This is the keystone of the whole edifice of materialistic philosophy. And here Lucretius writes:

> For verily not by design did the first beginnings of things station themselves each in its right place, guided by keen-sighted intelligence, nor did they bargain, sooth to say what motions each should assume, but because many in number, and shifting about in many ways throughout the universe, they are driven and tormented by blows during infinite time past; after trying motion and unions of every kind, at length they fall into arrangements such as those out of which this our sum of things has been formed, and by which too it is preserved through many great years, when once it has been thrown into the appropriate motions, and causes the streams to replenish the greedy sea with copious river-waters, and the earth, fostered by the heat of the sun, to renew its produce, and the race of living things to come up and flourish, and the gliding fires of ether to live.

In the Second Book Lucretius explains more fully the motion and the properties of atoms. They are, he declares, in everlasting movement, and this movement is originally a perpetual, equable falling through the boundless infinity of void space. He even proposes that the atoms must move in space with incomparably greater speed than the sun's rays.

Atoms are represented by Lucretius as extremely various in form. Now smooth and round, now rough and pointed, branched or hook-shaped, they exercise, according to their configuration, a particular influence upon our sense, or upon the properties of the bodies into whose composition they enter. The number of different forms is limited, but there are an unlimited number of each form, and in every body the most various atoms form special relationships with each other, and thus, by means of this combination, as in the combination of letters and words, an incomparably greater variety of bodies is possible than could otherwise result from the different shapes of the atoms.

In the midst of this passage he speaks again to the gods:

> And if anyone thinks proper to call the sea Neptune, and corn Ceres, and chooses rather to misuse the name of Bacchus (god of wine) than to utter the term that belongs to the liquor, let us allow him to declare that the earth is mother of the gods, if he only forbear in earnest to stain his mind with foul religion.

After Lucretius has further explained that color and the other sensible qualities do not proceed from the atoms themselves, but are only consequences of their operation in particular relations and combinations, he proceeds to the important question of the relation between sensation and matter. The fundamental position is that the sentient is developed out of the nonsentient. Lucretius holds to this fundamental position of materialism. He holds that it is not possible for sensation to proceed from anything under any circumstances, but that it depends on the shape, motion, and arrangement of matter, whether it shall produce the sentient or be capable of feeling. Sensation, he declares, is found only in the organic body and here belongs, not to the parts in themselves, but to the whole.

The proof that the sensation belongs not to the individual atoms but to the whole is adduced by Lucretius with some humor. It would not be a bad thing, he thinks, if human atoms could laugh and weep and speak sagely and ask what were their original constituent parts.

The sensation is to the entire individual, not to his atoms. But the sensation of the whole can in no case be a mere consequence of any possible functions of the individual, unless the whole also has a certain substantial reality, since out of an otherwise impossible summation of the nonsentience of the atoms, no sensation in the whole can arise.

The organic whole then was a new principle which Lucretius added to stand beside the idea of the atoms and the void.

In the Third Book of his poem, Lucretius summons all the forces of his philosophy to refute the doctrine of immortality, and he starts this by trying to rid us of the fear of death. When one sees a dead person, man knows that he himself must suffer the same. He does not realize that when he dies he cannot have two existences, the one of the body in the grave and the other of some continuing existence.

Nature itself is made to speak in his poem and proves to man the vanity of his fear of death. He reasserts that all that is known is life and that life and death are mutually exclusive; thus, we should concentrate on living.

The disappearance of the ancient civilizations, of Greece and of Rome, in the early centuries of the Christian era is an event the serious problems of which are in great part still unexplained. Everyone must rely on a few standard authors (Gibbon,[36] Lecky,[37] Draper,[38] Humboldt[39]). Actually we know this history only in bold strokes.

We do know that amidst the progress of reason and knowledge and method of both, the intellectual aristocracy broke away from the masses of people. The lack of popular education must have hastened and intensified this separation. The increasing intercourse of nations began to produce among the superstitious masses a confusion of religions, many of which were Oriental and Egyptian. In this welter, the philosophy of Aristotle came to be supreme; the religion of Christianity was everywhere established by the sword.

Progress could only come by shattering this system, in which were embodied the prejudices and fundamental errors of idealist philosophy. About the middle of the fifteenth century, Humanism entered upon its struggle against what was called Scholasticism, and everywhere was heard the lament, all in condemned doctrines:

Nothing more can be known, because of the science of theology.
The Christian religion prevents us from learning anything more.
The only wise men in the world are the philosophers.
The teachings of the theologians are based upon fables.

The bishops of the church attacked these attitudes everywhere, with vigor.

One man, particularly, Petrus Pomponatius, delivered perhaps the boldest and acutest attack upon immortality, in 1516, in Italy. In his *De immortalitate animi* he held that immortality does not imply the eternal

---

[36]Edward Gibbon (1737–1794), English historian.
[37]William Edward Hartpole Lecky (1838–1903), Irish historian and essayist.
[38]John William Draper (1811–1882), American scientist and author.
[39]Friedrich Wilhelm Karl Heinrich Alexander von Humboldt (1769–1859), German naturalist, traveler, and statesman.

separate existence of the individual soul, but that, as the soul is "the form of the body," as Aquinas had asserted, it must, by hypothesis, perish with the body; form apart from matter being unthinkable. The treatise was burnt at Venice and Pomponatius ran serious risk of death at the hands of the Roman Catholics, until he declared his adherence to the Roman Catholic faith.

Giordano Bruno

But the person who reinvested materialism with legitimacy at last was Giordano Bruno. He connected it with the Copernican theory that:

> . . . all fixed stars are suns, which extend in infinite number through space, and have in turn their invisible (to us) satellites which are related to them just as the earth is to the sun, or the moon to the earth.

He concluded:

> . . . the infinity of forms under which matter appears, it does not receive from another and something external, but produces them from itself and engenders them from its own bosom. Matter is not that *prope nihil* which some philosophers have wished to make it, and as to which they have so much contradicted each other; not that naked, mere empty capacity, without efficiency, completeness, and fact.

Bruno conceived matter as actual and active. This principle is materialistic.

Bruno had originally entered the order of the Dominicans,[40] in order to find leisure for his studies; but having become suspected of heresy, he was obliged to flee, and from that time forward his life was unsettled and marked by a long chain of persecutions and hostilities. He stayed in turn at Geneva, at Paris, in England, and in Germany, at last to venture on that fatal step of returning to his native land, Italy. In the year 1592, at Venice, he fell into the hands of the Inquisition.[41]

---

[40]Dominicans, order of friars founded by St. Dominic in 1215 and dedicated to preaching.

46

After many years' confinement, he was condemned at Rome, still unbowed, and firm in his convictions. After being degraded and ex- communicated, he was handed over to the secular authorities, with the request that they would "punish him mercifully as possible, and without shedding of blood," a well-known formula which meant that he was to be burnt. When his sentence was announced to him, he said: "I suspect that you pronounce this sentence with more fear than I receive it." On the February 17, 1600, he was burnt in the Campofiore at Rome.

He was burned because he held that:

Matter as the absolute includes within itself all forms and dimen- sions. But the infinity of forms under which matter appears is not accepted by her from another nor as it were only in outward ap- pearance, but she brings them forth from herself and bears them from her own womb.

But the charges which were brought against him had to do with the Trinity and the incarnation.[42] The informer against him charged that he denied the Trinity and the incarnation as well as transubstantiation;[43] that he charged Christ and the apostles with having deceived the peo- ple through alleged miracles; that all friars were asses defiling the earth by their hypocrisy, avarice, and evil life; and that religion should be re- placed with philosophy.

In all of the discussion concerned with materialism, reaching from six hundred years before Christ to sixteen hundred after Christ, there are consistent conclusions in the thinking of those who postulate what is called materialism.

The materialist holds that thought is produced by the brain and in no other way. He denies that brainless thoughts exist.

The materialist holds that consciousness is a function of the brain; that consciousness has never been found dissociated from the brain.

The materialist holds that matter was prior to thought, and would

---

[41]A former Roman Catholic tribunal for the discovery and punishment of heresy.

[42]The embodiment of a god in earthly form — as Jesus Christ.

[43]The idea that the bread and wine of communion is actually the blood and flesh of Jesus Christ.

exist if there were no thought to perceive it.

The materialist holds that real knowledge is built up out of images made upon the brain center by real objects. Thought is the result of certain kinds of nervous or cerebral processes — a material phenomenon. Knowledge depends upon external impressions.

The materialist is convinced that there was "no first cause" or "beginning" for the universe, but that it is eternal. He reasons this out as follows: "All things that are now always, in substance or in some form were; Matter is eternal; Energy is eternal."

The materialist holds that not only organic life had a natural origin and evolution, but that mind and consciousness are due to the same process. He contends that the mind is built up out of impressions received from the material world; that thought depends upon external impressions; that knowledge is composed of sense impressions, and that consciousness is the sum total of our sense impressions. He holds that without these sense impressions there could be no knowledge.

The materialist calls attention to the fact that the brain is a physical organ; that when parts of it are destroyed, their respective functions are destroyed with them. For instance, when the center controlling speech is destroyed, the power of speech no longer exists.

Without senses we should have no mind. Without nerve energy we should have no senses. Consequently when our senses fail to work our minds or souls have ceased to be. Science knows nothing of disembodied spirit.

Everything traced has been found to be materialistic. The physical laws of nature are always in operation. They do not step aside even for a moment to permit anything else, such a spirit, to rule. The materialist holds that there is no spiritual existence apart from the material body.

For those who speak of souls, or of life after death, "If man can live without a body, why was he ever encumbered with one? If man is immortal, why has each one not lived from the beginning of time?"

The universe consists of matter, that is, a substance without cause, without purpose, and originally without consciousness, and subject only to mechanical laws of attraction and repulsion, impact and pressure. Consciousness has been derived from this substance, and perishes with the dissolution of organic bodies.

Matter is the only immortal thing. When atoms in organic form, called man, dissociate, man is blotted out permanently.

The materialism of antiquity was, in its ripest form, directed immediately and openly against religion, the complete annihilation of which Lucretius considered to be the most important business of man.

The materialist of today says simply, "There is nothing outside Nature."

Perhaps one of the finest statements of the morality of materialism was written by Paul Heinrich Dietrich von Holbach,[44] in his *System of Nature*.[45] He says in a preface to that book:

Man is unhappy merely because he misunderstands nature. His mind is so infected by prejudices that one must almost believe him to be forever doomed to error; the chains of illusion in which he is so entangled from childhood have so grown upon him that he can only with the utmost trouble be again set free from them. Unhappily he struggles to rise above the visible world, and painful experiences constantly remind him of the futility of his attempts. Man disdained the study of nature to pursue after phantoms, that . . . dazzled him and drew him from the plain path of truth away from which he cannot attain happiness. It is therefore time to seek in nature remedies against the evils into which fanaticism has plunged us. There is but one truth and it cannot harm us. To error are due the grievous fetters by which tyrants and priests everywhere succeed in enchaining the nations; from error arose the bondage to which the nations are subject; from error the terrors of religion which brought about that men mouldered in fear, or fanatically throttled each other for chimeras. From error arose deep-rooted hatred and cruel persecutions; the continual bloodshed and the horrid tragedies of which earth must be made the theatre to serve the interests of heaven.

Let us try, therefore, to banish the mists of prejudice, and to inspire man with courage and respect for his reason! If there is any one who cannot dispense with these delusions, let him at least allow others to form their own ideas in their own way, and let him be convinced that for the inhabitants of earth, the important thing is to be just, benevolent, and peaceful.

In this scheme, nature is the great whole of which man is a part and

---

[44]Paul Heinrich Dietrich von Holbach, Baron (1723–1789), French philosopher, leading Atheist, and materialist.
[45]*Système de la Nature, ou Des Loix du Monde Physique et du Monde Moral* (London: 1777).

by which he is influenced. The beings that we place outside nature have always been the creatures of imagination. There does not and cannot exist anything beyond the sphere that includes all creatures. Man is a physical being, and his moral existence is only a special aspect of his physical nature, a particular mode of action due to his peculiar organization.

And that is just what the materialism of modern Atheism says, yet twenty-five hundred years later.

(This *History of Materialism* was originally issued as programs number 383 to 388 of the "American Atheist Radio Series," broadcast weekly in 1976 from March 6 through April 10 on KLBJ-AM radio, in Austin, Texas. The series was titled as follows: #383, *History of Materialism — Introduction*; #384, *Materialism: The Contribution of Demokritos*; #385, *Materialism: Protagoras*; #386, *Materialism: Epikuros*; #387, *Materialism: Lucretius*; #388, *Materialism: Bruno*.)

Biography of Jon G. Murray

J on G. Murray is the president and chief executive officer of a number of American Atheist corporations as well as of the American Atheist General Headquarters in Austin, Texas, a national conglomerate of organizations and efforts of that 7 to 9 percent of the citizens of the United States who eschew the idea of god.

Housed in the GHQ are the American Atheist Press, the *American Atheist* magazine, the American Atheist Women, the American Atheist Library and Archives, the "American Atheist Forum" for television and the "American Atheist Radio Series" broadcasting, the American Atheist membership organization, and United World Atheists. The beginnings of an American Atheist political party are being formulated in that institution, and others are projected, particularly American Atheist University. The multimillion-dollar complex has been under the management of Jon G, Murray since June 1975.

A graduate of the University of Texas, Mr. Murray's creative writing abilities quickly established him as associate editor of the *American Atheist* magazine, which is currently recognized as a dissident voice of importance in the field of state/church separation in the nation and as a positive aggressive voice for Atheism in the world.

Cosponsor of the World Atheist Meet of 1980, in collaboration with Lavanam, director of the Indian Atheist Centre of Vijayawada, India, he acted as a cochairman of that event in India. He coordinated the World Atheist Meet of 1983 in Helsinki, Finland, after which event he headed a delegation of Atheist groups in visiting the various centers of Atheism in the U.S.S.R. A recognized television personality, veteran of hundreds of radio talk shows, he has appeared as an Atheist spokesman in the United States on every major program of importance. His forte is in lecturing at universities and colleges, where young Americans can identify with this (also) young leader. Dignified but determined, humorous but not caustic, prepared on his own position, he routs his religious protagonists with well-placed and well-researched barbs.

Beginning in 1976, he has been called upon to make appearances in behalf of American Atheists throughout Europe, Canada, the Scandinavian countries, Japan, China, the U.S.S.R., and India.

Mr. Murray excels as an administrator, organizer, public speaker, writer, and proponent of state/church separation. He is the author of *Essays of an Activist Atheist*[1] and *Essays on American Atheism.*[2] In addition, he collaborated with Dr. O'Hair on *All the Questions You Ever Wanted to Ask American Atheist with All the Answers,*[3] which has become an Atheist best-seller and stock book.

Mr. Murray has been a colitigant in lawsuits to remove the phrase "In God We Trust" from the nation's currency and coins, to stop prayers in governmental institutions, to prohibit the display of religious artifacts in government buildings (particularly the crèche or nativity scene during the Christmas season), to force the governments of five Southern states to accept Atheists and agnostics for jury service, government offices or positions of public trust, and to stop the pope from holding a Roman Catholic mass, at taxpayer expense, on the citizen-owned Washington, D.C., mall. Currently he is in his own litigation to enjoin the Texas courts from requiring prospective jurors to be sworn into office with a god oath, and to remove the tax exemption from church and religious institutional real estate. Mr. Murray also was the coordinator for the first picketing of a pope in world history, in Chicago, Illinois, in 1979.

Mr. Murray is the coordinator of the annual national American Atheist conventions, now in their third decade, held at different locations throughout the United States.

---

[1]*Essays of an Atheist Activist* (Austin, Texas: American Atheist Press, 1980).
[2]*Essays on American Atheism,* vols. 1 and 2 (Austin, Texas: American Atheist Press, 1986).
[3]*All the Questions You Ever Wanted to Ask American Atheists With All the Answers,* 2d ed. (Austin, Texas: American Atheist Press, 1986).

Speaking at Indiana University in Pennsylvania, where he was sponsored by the Philosophy and Religious Studies Club, Mr. Murray described the effect of Christianity on Western culture as "the plague of unthinking belief." Holding religion as totally irrelevant to human life, he excoriated the use of such "nonsense" words as "soul, universe, prayer, god, heaven, hell, angels, and the like." He emphasized that all religions are an incident (also an accident) of time and place.

Mr. Murray holds that religious beliefs are largely inherited and stem from religiously illiterate parents indoctrinating their minor children into "intellectual nonsense." A child accepts irrational ideas from parents on whom the child is dependent and whom the child loves and is then burdened with them into adult life. In this area of thought, the child can never reach intellectual maturity.

Mr. Murray also points out the fallacy of the expression "born-again Christian," indicating that all persons are born as Atheists — that is to say, free from religion — and only become Methodists or Roman Catholics or Jews when they are taught "such religious nonsense" by their parents.

Index

Membership Application For American Atheists

Last name: _____ First name: _____
   Companion's name (if family or couple membership)
Last name: _____ First name: _____
Address: _____
City/State/Zip: _____

   This is to certify that I am/we are in agreement with the "Aims and Purposes" and the "Definitions" of American Atheists. I/We consider myself/ourselves to be Materialist or Non-theist (*i.e.*, A-theist) and I/we have, therefore, a particular interest in the separation of state and church and American Atheists' efforts on behalf of that principle.

   I/We usually identify myself/ourselves for public purposes as (check one):

☐ Atheist   ☐ Objectivist   ☐ Agnostic
☐ Freethinker   ☐ Ethical Culturist   ☐ Realist
☐ Humanist   ☐ Unitarian   ☐ I/We evade any re-
☐ Rationalist   ☐ Secularist   ply to a query
☐ Other: _____

   I am/We are, however, an Atheist(s) and I/we hereby make application for membership in American Atheists. Both dues and contributions are to a tax-exempt organization and I/we may claim these amounts as tax deductions on my/our income tax return(s). *(This application must be dated and signed by the applicant[s] to be accepted.)*

Signature _____ Date _____
Signature _____ Date _____

   Membership in American Atheists includes a subscription to the monthly journal *American Atheist* and the monthly *Insider's Newsletter* as well as all the other rights and privileges of membership. Please indicate your choice of membership dues:

☐ Life, $750   ☐ Individual, $50/year
☐ Couple Life, $1,000 (Please   ☐ Age 65 or over, $25/year
   give both names above.)   (Photocopy of ID required.)
☐ Sustaining, $150/year   ☐ Student, $20/year (Photo-
☐ Couple/Family, $75/year   copy of ID required.)
   (Please give all names
   above.)

Upon your acceptance into membership, you will receive a handsome gold embossed membership card, a membership certificate personally signed by Jon G. Murray, president of American Atheists, our special monthly *Insider's Newsletter* to keep you informed of the activities of American Atheists, and a subscription to *American Atheist*. Life members receive a specially embossed pen and pencil set; sustaining members receive a commemorative pen. Your name will be sent to the Chapter in your local area if there currently is one, and you will be contacted so you may become a part of the many local activities. Memberships and subscriptions are nonrefundable.

☐ I am/We are enclosing a check or money order for $ _____ payable
   to American Atheists
☐ Please charge my/our charge card for $ _____ . ☐ Visa or ☐ MasterCard
   Card # _____
   Bank Name _____
   Expiration date _____
   Signature _____

Return form to:
American Atheists, Inc., P. O. Box 140195, Austin, TX 78714-0195

"AIMS AND PURPOSES"

(as recorded in documents of incorporation)

AMERICAN ATHEISTS ARE ORGANIZED:

(1) to stimulate and promote freedom of thought and inquiry concerning religious beliefs, creeds, dogmas, tenets, rituals, and practices;

(2) to collect and disseminate information, data, and literature on all religions and promote a more thorough understanding of them, their origins, and their histories;

(3) to advocate, labor for, and promote in all lawful ways the complete and absolute separation of state and church;

(4) to advocate, labor for, and promote in all lawful ways the establishment and maintenance of a thoroughly secular system of education available to all;

(5) to encourage the development and public acceptance of a humane ethical system, stressing the mutual sympathy, understanding, and interdependence of all people and the corresponding responsibility of each individual in relation to society;

(6) to develop and propagate a social philosophy in which man is the central figure, who alone must be the source of strength, progress, and ideals for the well-being and happiness of humanity;

(7) to promote the study of the arts and sciences and of all problems affecting the maintenance, perpetuation, and enrichment of human (and other) life; and

(8) to engage in such social, educational, legal, and cultural activity as will be useful and beneficial to members of American Atheists and to society as a whole.

"DEFINITIONS"

Atheism is the *Weltanschauung* (comprehensive conception of the world and of total human life value systems) of persons who are *free* from theism — *i.e., free from* religion. It is predicated on ancient Greek Materialism.

American Atheism may be defined as the mental attitude that unreservedly accepts the supremacy of reason and aims at establishing a life-style and ethical outlook verifiable by experience and the scientific method, independent of all arbitrary assumptions of authority or creeds.

Materialism declares that the cosmos is devoid of immanent conscious purpose; that it is governed by its own inherent, immutable, and impersonal laws; that there is no supernatural interference in human life; that man — finding his resources within himself — can and must create his own destiny. Materialism restores to man his dignity and his intellectual integrity. It teaches that we must prize our life on earth and strive always to improve it. It holds that man is capable of creating a social system based on reason and justice. Materialism's "faith" is in man and man's ability to transform the world culture by his own efforts. This is a commitment which is in every essence life-asserting. It considers the struggle for progress as a moral obligation and impossible without noble ideas that inspire man to struggle and bold creative works. Materialism holds that humankind's potential for good and for an outreach to more fulfilling cultural development is, for all practical purposes, unlimited.

American Atheists is a nonpolitical, nonprofit, educational organization. Another of its functions is to act as a "watchdog" to challenge any attempted breach of what Thomas Jefferson called "the wall of separation between state and church," upon which principle our nation was founded.

Membership is open only to those who are in accord with the "Aims and Purposes" indicated above and who are Atheist Materialists. Membership in the national organization is a prerequisite for membership in state, county, city, or local chapters. Membership fee categories are reflected on the reverse side of this sheet (American Atheists Membership Application form).

American Atheists, Inc.
P. O. Box 140195
Austin, TX 78714-0195

Don't Miss The
American Atheist

Founded by the first lady of Atheism, Dr. Madalyn O'Hair, the *American Atheist* is the magazine of the modern Atheist.

From the latest deeds of Atheist activists to the last antics of the religious right, its articles run the gamut of issues important to Atheists. Skirmishes in the state/church separation battle, the life-style and history of Atheism, religious criticism, current events are all included in the focus of this journal. The nation's hottest topics — school prayer, abortion, creationism — are all covered in its pages from the Atheist's viewpoint.

This magazine's writers bring readers a unique spectrum of viewpoints from literally all over the world. Examples? One columnist offers glimpses into the religions of India. Another highlights the pain of women in the Arab world. Jon Murray, president of American Atheists, spotlights the progress of Atheism (and religion) in the United States.

So why miss any more of this fascinating magazine? Though it is free to members of American Atheists, it is also available to nonmembers on a subscription basis. Go ahead: Check off a box below and head into the wonderful world of Atheism.

□ Regular subscription, $25/12 issues

□ Sustaining subscription, $50/12 issues (tax-deductible)

□ Foreign subscription, $35/12 issues

□ Sample copy, $2

Name: _____

Address: _____

City/State/Zip: _____

□ I am enclosing a check or money order for $ _____ payable to American Atheists.

□ Please charge my □ Visa or □ MasterCard for $ _____ .

   Card # _____

   Bank Name _____

   Expiration date _____

   Signature _____

Return form to:
American Atheists, Inc., P. O. Box 140195, Austin, TX 78714-0195

OTHER BOOKS FROM AMERICAN ATHEIST PRESS

The Bible Handbook by G. W. Foote & W. P. Ball———————$9.00
  Everything is here: absurdities, indecencies, contradictions, unfulfilled
  prophecies, broken promises of god, obscenities, sadomasochisms,
  impossibilities. Paperback. 372 pp. Stock #5008.

Pagan Origins of the Christ Myth by John G. Jackson———————$4.00
  This is one of the American Atheist Press' best-selling books. No wonder,
  since it takes on the question most historians of the Roman Empire era
  have not had the guts to ask — did Christ exist? The answer is NO! Find
  out why. Stapled. 32 pp. Stock #5204.

Ingersoll the Magnificent by Joseph Lewis———————$10.00
  Twenty-four classic orations by Robert Ingersoll, nemesis of the nine-
  teenth-century American clergy, demolishing organized religion. Paperback. 342 pp. Stock #5216.

The Case against Religion by Dr. Albert Ellis———————$4.00
  Religion is a mental illness — and this famous psychiatrist proves it!
  Stapled. 57 pp. Stock #5096.

I Bought My First Six-Pack When I Was 35 by John Bryan———————$10.00
  A humorous look at sexual repression and the Mormon church by an ex-
  member. Paperback. 146 pp. Stock #5029.

Why I Left the Roman Catholic Church by Charles Davis———————$4.00
  A damning condemnation by the man who had risen to head the Roman
  Catholic church in England, then quit in disgust. Learn why. Stapled. 22
  pp. Stock #5080.

The Peril of Faith by Martin Bard———————$7.00
  Bard reviews the positive aspects of Atheism and the logical arguments
  for it. He also introduces the reader to some of the heroes of Atheism
  and to the nonreligious foundation of the United States. Paperback. 175
  pp. Stock #5012.

Unzipped: The Popes Bare All by Arthur Frederick Ide———————$8.00
  A dispassionate, documented, and devastatingly detailed examination of
  all the gluttons, rapists, necrophiliacs, hedonists, slave-owners, pedophil-
  iacs, tyrants, murderers, and drug abusers presented by the Roman
  Catholic church as its Vicars of Christ. Paperback. 189 pp. Stock #5510.

The Great Infidels by Robert G. Ingersoll———————$6.00
  How nonbelievers and Atheists have contributed to civilization and
  enriched our lives. Paperback. 64 pp. Stock #5197.

Please add $2.50 postage and handling on all orders under $10. For orders over
$10, please add $3.50. VISA and MasterCard accepted.

(Texas residents please add applicable sales tax.)

Order from:

American Atheist Press, P. O. Box 140195, Austin, TX 78714-0195

OTHER BOOKS BY MADALYN O'HAIR

All the Questions You Ever Wanted to Ask American Atheists — with All the Answers by Madalyn O'Hair & Jon G. Murray
   The experience of 20 years of Atheist work is distilled into this 248-page paperback. Stock #5356. $9.00.

Women and Atheism: The Ultimate Liberation
   This is the unexpurgated chapter of *Freedom Under Siege,* which was seriously censored in that publication. The full story of Christianity's oppression, suppression, and repression of women. Paperback. 21 pp. Stock #5420. $3.50.

Atheist Primer
   Gods are figments of human imagination. This fact is clearly and humorously explained in simple language a small child can easily understand. Illustrated children's book. Paperback. 30 pp. Stock #5372. $4.00.

What on Earth Is an Atheist!
   This book of essays looks at church wealth and businesses, materialism, the Christian Bible, and other subjects. Paperback. 288 pp. Stock #5412. $8.00.

An Atheist Speaks
   Madalyn O'Hair explores the deism of the Founding Fathers, analyzes the tax exemptions given to churches, reports on Atheist Margaret Sanders, and examines the dangers of exposing children to religion — and lots more. Paperback. 322 pp. Stock #5098. $8.00.

All about Atheists
   Though this work focuses on the history of Atheism, in a series of essays, Madalyn O'Hair touches on many other subjects. They include the atrocities of the Bible, the zodiac, and letters from Christians. Paperback. 407 pp. Stock #5097. $8.00.

Our Constitution: The Way It Was
   Beginning with an examination of the religious oppression present in the Colonies, Madalyn O'Hair recounts the Founding Fathers' determination to erect a wall of separation between state and church. Stapled. 70 pp. Stock #5400. $4.00.

Atheists: The Last Minority
   The plight of being an Atheist in a theist society is examined in this reprint of a 1990 speech aired on C-SPAN. Stapled. 24 pp. Stock #5402. $3.00.

Please add $2.50 postage and handling on all orders under $10. For orders over $10, please add $3.50. VISA and MasterCard accepted.
   (Texas residents please add applicable sales tax.)

Order from:
**American Atheist Press, P. O. Box 140195, Austin, TX 78714-0195
Telephone orders: (512) 467-9525**

An Atheist Epic
by Madalyn O'Hair

On June 14, 1954, the Pledge of Allegiance was changed to include the words "under God."

On July 11, 1955, President Eisenhower made the slogan "In God We Trust" mandatory on all currency. The national motto was changed to the same god phrase on July 30, 1956.

And in 1959 a self-admitted Atheist challenged school prayer.

The 1950s — it was the decade of "Father Knows Best" and the Red Scare. A good American was a Christian American — or at least a religious one. The enemy was "godless communism," and our best weapon against it was the Christianization of America.

But a Baltimore woman challenged all that.

She simply said "no" to mandatory prayer — and started a controversy that still rages today.

That woman was Madalyn Murray. And *An Atheist Epic* is her story, from the first complaint to the public school that required her child to say the Lord's Prayer to the day the Supreme Court gave its decision in the landmark school prayer case *Murray v. Curlett*. New edition; now includes photos.

302 pp. Paperback. Stock #5376.

$10.00 plus $3.00 postage and handling per book.

DATE DUE

OCT 26 1994			
OCT 21 1999			